Postsecondary Participation and State Policy

Stylus Higher Education Policy Series

Higher education is facing fundamental questions about financing, affordability, access, quality, outcomes, and diversity. College and university administrators, as well as state and federal policymakers, need reliable data, effective interpretation of research, innovative ideas, and cogent analysis to guide them in the critical decisions they will be facing in the near and long term.

The series aims to bring together the nation's most respected researchers, scholars, and policy analysts to inform the debate on these issues, and help shape future policy.

Series Editor: Donald E. Heller, Associate Professor and Senior Research Associate at the Center for the Study of Higher Education, The Pennsylvania State University.

Submissions: The Editor and Publisher welcome proposals for volumes in the series. E-mail dheller@psu.edu

Postsecondary Participation and State Policy
Meeting the Future Demand

Mario Martinez

STERLING, VIRGINIA

Published in 2004 by

Stylus Publishing, LLC
22883 Quicksilver Drive
Sterling, Virginia 20166

Copyright © 2004 Stylus Publishing, LLC

All rights reserved. No part of this book may be reprinted or reproduced in any form or by any electronic, mechanical or other means, now known or hereafter invented, including photocopying, recording and information storage and retrieval, without permission in writing from the publishers.

Library of Congress Cataloging-in-Publication Data
Martinez, Mario, 1967–
   Postsecondary participation and state
     policy : meeting the future demand /
     Mario Martinez.—1st ed.
       p. cm.—(Stylus higher education
        policy series)
   Includes bibliographical references and
     index.
   ISBN 1-57922-116-5 (hardcover : alk.
paper)—ISBN 1-57922-117-3
(pbk. : alk paper)
   1. Postsecondary education—Government
policy—United States. 2. Higher
education and state—United States.
3. Universities and colleges—United
States—States—Admission. I. Title.
II. Series.
LC173.M293 2004
379.1'224'0973—dc22
                   2004000455

First edition, 2002
ISBN: hardcover 1-57922-116-5
      paperback 1-57922-117-3

Printed in the United States of America
All first editions printed on acid free paper

To my wife, Sara

For all your support, your logical reasoning, and our many conversations that challenge me and help shape my thoughts.

Contents

FOREWORD	xi
PREFACE	xix
INTRODUCTION	1
Demographics and Policy	4
1. THE IMPORTANCE OF POSTSECONDARY PARTICIPATION	7
The Benefits of Higher Education: Past and Present	8
The Growing Case for Postsecondary Participation	10
2. THE CURRENT STATE OF POSTSECONDARY PARTICIPATION	15
The Current Picture of Postsecondary Participation	15
Population by Age	18
Applying Financial Ratio Analysis to Postsecondary Participation	20
18- to 24-Year-Olds	23
25 and Older	27
Conclusion	30
3. THE FUTURE STATE OF POSTSECONDARY PARTICIPATION	31
2015 Age Group Populations	34
Comparison Ratio Changes	42
Conclusion	45

4. LEAVE NO STUDENT BEHIND: EXCEEDING
   THE STATUS QUO   47
   Benchmark Achievement   49
   Moving Toward Improvement   54
   Baseline Plus   55
   Conclusion   59

5. FUNDING HIGHER EDUCATION
   IN THE FUTURE   61
   Enrollment Growth   63
   The Inflation Factor   66
   Future Funding Scenarios   68
   Conclusion   74

6. STATE POLICY AND HIGHER
   EDUCATION SUPPLY   77
   Successful State Policy in the Future   80
   Conclusion   88

7. ALIGNING POLICYMAKER EXPECTATIONS
   WITH FUTURE DEMAND   91
   Outcomes   91
   Means and Ends   92
   Changing Demographics and Higher Education Policy   94
   Achieving Outcomes   99
   Conclusion   101

APPENDIXES
   A. 2000 Participation Statistics, with Participation Rates 103
   B. 2000 Participation Statistics, with Comparison Ratios   106
   C. 2015 Population Statistics   109
   D. 2015 Participation Statistics   112
   E. Enrollment Changes: 2000 to 2015   115
   F. 2015 Comparison Ratios   118
   G. 2015 Projected Enrollments: 18–24   121
   H. 2015 Projected Enrollments: 25+   124

I.	2015 Projected Enrollments: 18+	127
J.	Enrollment Growth Factors	130
K.	Funding Scenarios	132
L.	Appropriation Increases	134
M.	2000 Appropriations	137

REFERENCES 139

NOTES 143

INDEX 147

Foreword

Mario Martinez gives us fair warning. He demonstrates with irrefutable statistical evidence that the first decades of the new century present unprecedented challenges as well as new opportunities for achieving access and equity in higher education. While no one can predict the future precisely, he points out demographic and economic realities already in place that suggest the shape of things to come.

Martinez addresses national trends but takes his policy analysis to the state level. He points out that state histories, cultures, and political makeup, as well as different demographic and economic trajectories, will make huge differences in higher education policy alternatives. Demographic change will be very uneven. Essentially, every state with a beach or with an increasing Hispanic population from Massachusetts to Washington will see rising student populations. Institutions matter as well, and this issue is also addressed in the book. States with well-developed community college systems should be able to provide greater accessibility to higher education for both youths and adults.

As Martinez demonstrates, states are the fulcrum for higher education policy. He also recognizes that there are a common set of national demographic and economic trends that provide the context for state variations and a set of persistent policy concerns for access and choice in higher education that are not affected by state boundaries. Demography provides the rigorous core of Martinez's narrative. The Census Bureau population projections indicate a major expansion in demand for seats in higher education over the next decade. In Martinez's projections, the size of the core client base of 18- to 24-year-olds is projected to rise by 4 million youth to a total of 30 million 18- to 24-year-olds by 2015. If current participation rates continue, the increase of over 4 million traditional college-age students should result in an expansion in college enrollment by about 1.2 million students by 2015. The imminent boom in the traditional college-age population reflects the maturation of "Generation Y," or the "baby-boom echo." Referring to youth born between 1982 and 1997, the heart of Generation Y (those born between 1989 and 1993) will reach age 18 in 2007. The end of the Generation Y bulge will hit age 24 in 2017. This increase only accounts for enrollment among 18- to 24-year-olds. The number of nontraditional students 25 and older also should increase. Martinez calculates that at current participation rates the number of students 25 and older will increase by more than a million by 2015.

Demography and the Economic Demand for College-Educated Workers

While economics cannot claim the same level of certainty as demography, economic trends are reasonably clear. Changes in the structure of work over the past half century have made access to education and training after high school the threshold requirement for landing a middle-class job. Since 1979, the economic premium paid to workers with at least some college has increased from 42 to 62 percent, even as the supply of workers with at least some college has doubled as a share of all workers. Workers who receive at least some postsecondary education but no degree, an associate degree, a bachelor's degree, or graduate education have immediate earnings advantages over high school graduates of 14, 30, 73, and 120 percent, respectively.

The combined effect of upcoming baby-boom retirements and restructuring in favor of skilled jobs suggests that there may not be enough college-educated workers in the future. Overall growth in the labor force is expected to decline from an increase of 50 percent between 1980 and 2000 (about 40 million workers), to a growth rate of only 16 percent between 2000 and 2020. The increase in the share of workers with postsecondary education will be relatively flat between 2000 and 2020, but jobs requiring at least some college will continue to grow by almost 35 percent.

All other things equal, in combination, the mix of demographic and economic trends could result in a shortage of as many as 14 million workers with at least some college by 2020. These projections should make readers more comfortable with Martinez's most expansive standard for postsecondary access. Martinez bases his upper-bound benchmark for increasing higher education participation on current participation rates in Rhode Island and California—the states with the nation's highest participation rates for traditional and nontraditional students, respectively. Rhode Island has the highest participation rate among 18- to 24-year-olds at 48 percent, and California has the highest participation rated among those over the age of 25 at 6 percent. If all states had participation rates as high as California and Rhode Island, there would be an increase in participation of roughly 4 million

18- to 24-year-olds, and 4 million students over the age of 25. An increase of 8 million students by 2015 seems like a worthy goal in an economy that could absorb an additional 14 million people with at least some college by 2020.

Academic Preparation

Demography guarantees a growing number of high school graduates, and best estimates suggest that the economy can absorb a growing number of college-educated workers. But will future high school graduates be prepared for college? While we can't determine future performance, we can examine how K–12 students are doing in school compared to past generations. Martinez offers different participation scenarios for the future precisely because factors such as K–12 performance and high school graduation rates influence postsecondary participation. His identification of such issues is simply an invitation to pursue additional analysis that will be meaningful for the nation and states.

For example, the National Assessment of Education Progress (NAEP), often referred to as the "nation's report card," provides the most nationally representative indicator of the academic skills of our nation's youth still in the K–12 system. By matching up the NAEP results for Generation Y to earlier cohorts at the same age, we can compare the current students in the education pipeline with those who have gone before. The latest NAEP long-term trend assessment (conducted in 1999) provides results on mathematics, reading, and science abilities for 9-year-olds—those who were born in 1990 and are in the heart of Generation Y. These 9-year-olds performed somewhat better than earlier cohorts, and performed significantly better in all subject areas than their baby-boomer parents (who took the assessment as 9-year-olds in the early 1970s). As a result, it seems safe to expect that we can easily maintain the current participation rates Martinez identifies. Even better, if present trends in K–12 performance continue, a growing share of college-qualified students in an expanding 18- to 24-year-old cohort should increase the number of college-qualified students significantly by 2015.

But what about minority students? Roughly 80 percent of the 4 million plus expansion in the traditional college-age population expected by 2015 will be minority youth. About half the coming boom in the 18- to 24-year-old population will be Hispanic. In addition, about 680,000 of the new 18- to 24-year-olds will be African Americans and 80,000 will be Native Americans.

Due to the well-known gaps between non-Hispanic White children and minority children on achievement tests, combined with the growing proportion of minority children over time, concerns have been raised that Generation Y may be less academically prepared to enter and succeed in college than earlier generations. But the available evidence suggests the concerns over the rising share of minority students in the K–12 system are overstated and can be destructive if they lead to reduced expectations and declining policy support for minority access. In fact, the demographics of the next decade offer a unique window of opportunity for minority inclusion through higher education. Early test results from the NAEP and other sources suggest that the current share of minority students ready for college will actually grow slightly. The new cohorts of minority students will be at least as well prepared as previous minority cohorts. This means that as minority students become a growing proportion of the 18- to 24-year-olds, the share of minority students ready to go on to college should increase steadily and the number of college-qualified minorities should increase substantially.

In sum, there is evidence that a growing number of 18- to 24-year-olds, including minorities, will be college ready. Such evidence underscores the importance of examining the future demand for postsecondary education and the fiscal challenges that states are likely to face along the way.

Funding the Benefits of Higher Education

The economic and demographic demand for higher education will continue to grow. In a pure economic market with no income constraints, these conditions would be a recipe for efficient and equitable expansion. But for the most part, American higher education is publicly funded and regulated. Martinez thus looks at the corresponding state funding obligations that will be required to meet increasing postsecondary participation. These fiscal projections give rise to a host of public policy questions that states must consider as they plan for the future: Will the states be able to meet the financial obligations for funding higher education in the future? How much should the student pay? Can access across age and race be maintained or improved?

Private and public costs of college should be expected to expand with overall economic growth, especially when the economic returns to college are growing and when the college-age population grows. As the economy grows, individuals consume more college education in the interest of personal development and exploration. Individuals should pay for what they consume privately. And as the private economic returns to postsecondary education rise, so should investments in postsecondary education. And the costs of college that bring economic returns should be paid by individuals and institutions that capture them, either directly or by borrowing against future income generated from postsecondary investments.

The book outlines the private benefits of a college education and the importance that participation plays in starting that process, but the author also reviews the broadly shared public benefits from increases in access to college that available data suggest are even greater than private returns to individuals. Social benefits of this kind include improvements to the general welfare from increased social and economic mobility and more robust civic participation to the benefits from postsecondary contributions to cultural criticism, cultural transmission, and cultural enrichment. There also are broadly disseminated economic returns from increases in the overall stock of college-educated workers that exceed the sum of individual returns to college. In addition, a more highly educated population is more receptive to new technologies and more agile in adapting to economic change.

In the current context, spending per capita for higher education has barely kept pace with economic growth. In concept, increasing public and private economic returns, along with the increasing consumption that accompanies increasing wealth, suggest that higher education spending should be growing faster than the economy. This has not been the case, so Martinez's state funding projections of what it would take to meet the future demand for higher education serve as an important reminder of how far we have to go.

The decline in state support for higher education raises important concerns, especially when viewed in light of the author's state funding projections. Since 1990, states have been cutting taxes and reducing commitments to higher education. While the actual dollar amounts from state budgets going to higher education increased consistently from the 1980s up until the 2001 recession, between 1990 and 2000, the share of state budgets going to colleges has fallen off by 15 percent. State tax cuts could account for roughly half of the decline in state support for postsecondary education, but the other half is due to rapidly rising state spending for medicaid and prisons. The share of state budgets going to medicaid has doubled from 8 to 16 percent, and the share going to prisons has increased by one-third. Consequently, the largest source of new revenue for colleges has come from rising tuitions, which have increased by more than 110 percent since 1980. These trends point to the serious attention that policymakers must give to higher education policy if states are going reach the ideal participation rates given in this book.

Avoiding the Access Illusion

Martinez clearly shows that demographic trends in the states will vary: some states will see their traditional 18- to 24-year-old population increase at a faster rate than the 25 and older population, but in many other states the opposite will be true. These trends should figure into how states plan and prepare for the future.

Historically, as money gets tighter, the traditional upper-middle-class 18- to 24-year-old students become the preferred clients. These students arrive with tuition in hand, are assembled on campus, sit in large classes scheduled during normal working hours, and are taught standardized academic curricula. The least attractive clients are the adults with work and family responsibilities. Low-income students and adults require more expensive courses that mix applied and academic learning; flexible scheduling that increases personnel and facilities costs; and family services, such as child care and counseling, to hold it all together and plan for future transitions. Low-income students and adults also may require remedial or refresher courses that no one wants to pay for, along with customized work-oriented courses that oftentimes need to be offered in bite-sized, non-degreed chunks that are not eligible for federal subsidies and are only funded, in part, by a minority of states.

Indeed, each state will need to examine the specifics of its population growth and offer appropriate postsecondary services to be economically, socially, and politically successful. After all the demographic evidence is laid out in the book, specific state examples demonstrate how the dynamic of population growth might influence the services that states emphasize to meet the future demand for postsecondary education. With increasing financial pressures, the increase in higher education access, in general, and campus diversity, in particular, may become more apparent than real. For example, demographic momentum from the surge in the 18- to 24-year-olds through 2015 virtually ensures increased enrollments but not increases in the share of 18- to 24-year-olds enrolled, which is a better measure of access.

In this book, Mario Martinez describes profound structural changes that will ensure equally profound changes in American higher education. These structural changes require structural solutions far beyond the grasp of our current political stalemate and retail politics. Rising tuitions are just one more public problem that track to larger structural changes in our economy, in our demography, and in the changing roles of public institutions. Ultimately, the question is not whether we spend too much or too little on higher education but whether spending is efficiently and equitably aligned between public and private purposes.

The question of college access and quality will remain with us because the economic and demographic forces that drive it are relentless. This book tracks both of these forces and raises issues to help those interested in the future of higher education think about the future of access and quality in the states. Young people aren't going anywhere in today's economy unless they get at least some postsecondary education or training first. As a result, earnings differences between college haves and have-nots will continue to increase. In an economy where good jobs require access to postsecondary education and training, the already growing economic divide between adults with and without postsecondary education and training will continue to widen, fostering intergenerational reproduction of economic and cultural elites inimical to our democratic ethos and our worthiness for leadership in the global contest of cultures.

Anthony P. Carnevale
Vice President, Educational Testing Service

Preface

This book is largely the result of my participation on a project with the Education Commission of the States. The ECS was interested in looking at state-by-state participation and asked me if I would help mine national data sources for credible information on state postsecondary education. Sandra Ruppert, in particular, asked me if I would join the effort, and she was very supportive of using information from the project as a major input for this book. Sandra has been a longtime colleague with whom I have shared a common interest in state higher education policy and legislative perspectives. Her work at the ECS has gained national visibility because of her ability to fuse legislative input with issues important to the future of higher education. I am obviously indebted to Sandra for encouraging me to pursue this book, for making information from her previous work available to me, and for providing feedback on the manuscript. I would like to thank Don Heller, who was the person who listened to my idea and allowed me to pursue it. Don is a national voice on issues important to higher education policy, and he saw the need for this book and facilitated my work with Stylus to bring the manuscript to fruition. Michelle Nilson edited the manuscript, created the index, and provided critical feedback that helped organize and shape the final product. I am grateful for her positive attitude and her substantive contributions. Gary Ivory and Mimi Wolverton are longtime colleagues and friends, and for their continued moral support and encouragement I thank them.

Mario C. Martinez
January 2004

Introduction

Americans want access to higher education[a]—for themselves and for their children. The 25 and older population is increasingly searching for education and training opportunities after years and even decades of work experience. Parents want their children to go to college and be a part of an experience that will help them find satisfying employment and a better quality of life. In a recent national survey, Immerwahr and Foleno (2000) found that Americans across all racial and ethnic groups overwhelmingly see higher education as essential for success.

It seems ironic, then, that the issue of how states can maximize access to higher education receives so little public debate and policy discussion. Callan and Finney (1997) point out that we would be hard pressed to find two areas outside of higher education access and finance that have undergone such significant change without public discussion or explicit policy direction. The imperative is made even greater by the projected growth in demand for higher education over the next decade.

The dissonance between what Americans hope for and the lack of discussion at the policy level is the impetus for this book. This volume examines current postsecondary participation, projections of future demand, and the funding needs that will be required to meet future demand. The demographic-based information and analysis throughout the book are intended to stimulate discussion about higher education policy in the states. An informed policy discussion, grounded in credible data, gives rise to different policy alternatives to address the access challenges that states are likely to face. A policy alternative that is effective in one state may not be effective in another. It is the combination of each state's unique history, current priorities, and prospects for the future that will dictate which alternative policymakers are likely to favor. The book's goal is not to definitively suggest that one policy option is superior to another. The aim is to stimulate an informed discussion about policy alternatives that might maximize higher education access. Policy that is based on information, discussion, and legitimate debate avoids what Callan and Finney (1997) describe as a "policy vacuum."

The U.S. 2000 decennial census, disaggregated by age and state, serves as the primary data source to profile current postsecondary participation in the initial chapters. The decennial census provides standardized information for all 50 states and the nation across a number of social, economic, and education parameters. The decennial census is conducted once every 10 years via in-depth household surveys that are based on self-reported information. The resulting data sets are considered to be among the most comprehensive, credible, and easily accessible data sources assembled by the U.S. government. These three characteristics make it a logical choice upon which to base an analysis of state postsecondary participation. United States Census 2000 decennial data, by state, became publicly available in September 2002.

The 2000 decennial census data also provide various social, economic, and education indicators across the states by race and ethnicity. However, state-by-state census postsecondary participation data by race and ethnicity are limited compared to participation data by age. Additionally, there exist some concerns about the accuracy of projecting into the future using race and ethnicity, namely the difficulty of accounting for interracial marriages (Perlmann & Waters, 2002) and immigration.

Future enrollment projections in Chapters 3 and 4 rely on census demographic projections for 2015 by age. State-by-state projections by age are readily available for 2015. These projections can be used to estimate future enrollment, which can then be compared to current postsecondary participation statistics. The census also provides detailed state population projections by age for 2010, 2020, and 2025. For this book, the 2015 projections serve as the focal point because 2015 is far enough into the future to encourage forward thinking and close enough to the present that it includes the majority of today's adults and children.

Access will be affected by a number of social, political, and demographic factors in the future. The focus in this book on the demographic factor of age allows a level of specificity that will be meaningful to states. It also provides the Key Issues in Higher Education Series a starting point to raise core issues related to higher education access and funding. This focus does not dismiss the relative importance of other factors and their effect on participation. Subsequent investigations that detail state-by-state projections by race and ethnicity or income and gender would be valuable complements to this volume.

The chapters primarily focus on two age groups: 18- to 24-year-olds and those 25 and older. Statistics show a small percentage of persons under the age of 18 who are enrolled in some form of postsecondary credit, but that percentage is nominal and not included in this analysis.[1] The traditional student population is captured in the 18- to 24-year-old population, and tracking this population remains critical for all states. Census projections indicate that several states, including California, New Jersey, and New York, will experience large increases in their 18- to 24-year-old populations between now and 2015.

The second student population includes people 25 and older. This group is commonly referred to as the adult student population. The adult student population has historically drawn less attention than the traditional student population. The demand for access from students 25 and older is likely to increase in most states between now and 2015. Virtually every state in the nation will experience a population increase for this age group. States such as Arkansas and Idaho will experience a dramatic surge in the 25 and older population over the next several years. There are already a number of states in which the total number of adult students is greater than the traditional student population. Indeed, in many states, the age group that is in the minority today may be in the majority tomorrow.

Although the foundation of the analysis is participation by age, as provided by census data, other sources serve as a supplement when appropriate. Supplementary sources sometimes provide additional detail not found in census data and are employed to the extent that they help provide a more complete picture of postsecondary participation. Participation by sector and level, for example, details the percentage of a state's enrollment at public and private institutions, both two- and four-year. For many states, the appropriate mix of public and private institutions, both two- and four-year, plays or will play a central role in decisions about access, funding, and governance.

Postsecondary participation is examined at both the national and state levels throughout the book. Select states are highlighted in tables and graphics throughout the text to illustrate variations across different measures of participation, but all 50 states are included in the appendixes. Policymakers are often interested in looking at other states or viewing their state against a national average; thus states are often compared on the basis of regionalism, size, age demographics, or other measures. The approach here is to demonstrate how states vary across the different measures of postsecondary participation. Benchmarks and national averages are provided to establish standards for comparison. States may choose to use the benchmark or national average as a basis for comparison, or they may establish their own criteria for comparison.

State variations across certain measures of performance may point to differences in state characteristics that are not easily or immediately controlled by state policy or institutional action. A state's racial, ethnic, economic, geographic, historical, or even religious climate—hereafter referred to as state context—may influence postsecondary participation. Three independent studies (Martinez, Farias, & Arellano, 2002; Cunningham & Wellman, 2001; NCPPHE, 2000) confirm that state context explains some of the variation across different measures of higher education performance (including participation), though certainly not all of it.

The importance of these studies is twofold. First, since state context only explains a portion of performance variation, there is a strong indication that state policy matters in the long run. Second, state context cannot be completely ignored and should be taken into account when looking at variations in higher education performance within and across states. The different measures of current postsecondary participation will allow state-by-state comparison while being sensitive to state context when it is clear that such context is in some way impacting performance.

Demographics and Policy

The dynamic of population changes in the states will likely lead to different strategies for maximizing access to higher education. The value of examining current enrollment against projected enrollment is that the magnitude of the difference can inform policy discussions aimed at improving higher education access. In addition, demographic projections by state are far more meaningful than a national analysis by itself. National analysis, while useful, can mask significant state variation and thus may be of little use to the states. The shifts and changes among states are rarely reflected in a national statistic. There is a danger of assuming that little has changed in the states if the national average on a given measure shows little change.

As current and future enrollment differences surface, questions concerning resource needs emerge. Any trend impacted by demographic changes has implications for state spending, and future higher education access is such a trend. Policymakers must simultaneously examine the many services that a state must provide against available or projected resources. Another component of the book, therefore, addresses the possible fiscal impact of future enrollment demand on state budgets.

Future and past state budgets are often assessed against two variables: demographics and inflation. Consultants, government officials, and even the popular media often conduct such assessments. During the height of the states' budget crises in 2003, for example, *USA Today* (Cauchon, 2003) conducted an in-depth analysis to determine how well the states were managed. One aspect of the study assessed whether past state spending was fiscally wise and restrained. This past spending was adjusted for demographic and inflation changes. Funding projections should also account for assumptions of inflation and demography. In Chapter 5, the funding projections that accompany the future enrollment scenarios account for both inflation and demographic changes.

The projected demand for higher education will have an important impact on state higher education policy in the future and is therefore a central theme of the later chapters. In several national surveys, policymakers have also given an indication of their expectations for higher education. These expectations will be compared against future enrollment and funding projections. Seven chapters guide the analysis and discussion:

- Chapter 1, "The Importance of Postsecondary Participation":

  Why is it important to compare current and future enrollments? What is the benefit of access to higher education, and why is it important to the state, to policymakers, and to individual citizens?

- Chapter 2, "The Current State of Postsecondary Participation":

  Current participation rates are calculated for 18- to 24-year-olds and those 25 and older, using 2000 decennial census data. Additional demographic information is analyzed relative to participation rates to provide an expanded view of postsecondary education in the states.

- Chapter 3, "The Future State of Postsecondary Participation":

  Projected demographic changes in the two age groups are coupled with current state participation rates to offer a view of the expected demand for higher education in 2015.

- Chapter 4, "Leave No Student Behind: Exceeding the Status Quo":

  Projected demographic changes in the two age groups are coupled with assumptions of improved state participation rates to offer additional scenarios of higher education demand in 2015. These assumptions yield demand projections that go beyond the status quo enrollment scenario presented in the previous chapter.

- Chapter 5, "Funding Higher Education in the Future":

Demography and inflation impact state budgets over time. This chapter considers the various future enrollment scenarios from the previous chapters and their associated impact on state budgets.

- Chapter 6, "State Policy and Higher Education Supply":

  State policy influences higher education supply and demand. The focus of this chapter is on state policies that expand access by expanding supply. Policy alternatives are discussed in the context of demographic changes.

- Chapter 7, "Aligning Policymaker Expectations with Future Demand":

  The expectations that policymakers have of higher education are outlined in this chapter. Six states illustrate how demographic patterns could be used to formulate policies in the future and meet legislative expectations.

In each chapter there is information that policymakers have indicated is important to the future of their states. Policymaker input is most prominent in Chapters 1 and 7. The bulk of this input is taken from two comprehensive national surveys with state legislators. Sandra Ruppert published the first survey in 1996 and the second in 2001. The focus of the two surveys was on higher education policy, and each survey asked for policymaker input on a range of issues related to current and future postsecondary education across the states. Both surveys contain information that is critical to any commentary on higher education policy. Ruppert served as a key advisor to this project since her work is so strongly reflected in it.

Legislators attach great importance to state higher education and believe it is tied to the health of their states and individual opportunity. A demographic comparison of current postsecondary participation and future enrollment projections simply emphasizes the need to pursue policies that might enhance access in the years ahead.

CHAPTER 1

The Importance of Postsecondary Participation

Much has been written about the benefits of higher education. Few would dispute the connection between higher education and certain individual and social benefits, but several questions remain. Does higher education result in more individual or social benefits? When do the benefits of higher education surface, at entry into an institution or upon successful degree completion? The significance of these questions will rise as the demand for higher education escalates and the competition for state resources intensifies.

This chapter first documents the public and private benefits associated with higher education. The second part of the chapter presents empirical evidence linking postsecondary participation and educational attainment to public and private benefits. Participation, learning, and degree completion all contribute to the many benefits associated with higher education, and each is important to the production of those benefits. Intuitively, participation, learning, and degree completion are related, but the focus in this chapter is on participation and its relationship to degree attainment and higher education benefits. There is evidence that suggests participation is a reasonable starting point for policymakers to empirically measure and target progress toward the betterment of their states. Studies that emphasize public and private benefits as a result of learning and completion should be seen as a complement to this work.

The Benefits of Higher Education: Past and Present

In American colonial times, higher education was only available to the elite members of society. There was little debate as to who should have access to higher education. Much was written, however, about why higher education was so important—the benefits of a college education. Bowen (1977) notes that several early writers, including people like Thomas Jefferson and John Stuart Mill, believed that higher education's goal was more about growth and development than skill and knowledge acquisition. Bowen provides a summary of the intended outcomes of higher education that powerfully outlines the historical beliefs about the benefits of providing higher education to a society and its people: society gains qualified and credible individuals to govern states and run businesses, schools, and civic organizations; and individuals gain income, job satisfaction, and life experiences that inform the personal decisions they make for the rest of their lives. Those benefits are still applicable today and will continue to be in the future.

Bloom (1987) articulated what can be considered the ultimate individual benefit of higher education. He described higher education as a ticket to the good life because those who obtain it have entrée to the economic, cultural, and social benefits that society has to offer. The Texas Higher Education Coordinating Board's opening statement, in its report *Closing the Gap* (2002), reminds us that individual and social benefits accrue as citizens participate in postsecondary education and complete degrees:

> Higher education is a great benefit to both individual and society. People with a college education earn larger salaries and see greater financial benefits over their lifetimes. They also have greater job satisfaction and employment opportunities, and are more likely to give back to their communities. Their higher earnings contribute to the state's economic base through taxes and they are less likely to require public assistance. (p. 4)

The production of public and private benefits for more Americans began in earnest in the middle of the 20th century. The country began to shift its thinking about "who" should have access to higher education. The 1947 President's Commission on Higher Education paved the way for broader access to higher education. The creation of the GI Bill and Pell Grant program made higher education available to more people and opened the door to those who would not have been able to afford college on their own. Recent polls confirm that an overwhelming majority of Americans believe that all motivated and qualified individuals should have the opportunity to attend college, regardless of race, ethnicity, income, or background. The challenge for states today is "how" to provide that access in a climate of resource constraint and competition for funds.

States have to make choices about how much to appropriate to institutions and students. States must also decide how to allocate funds and whether there are any criteria for receiving them. Inherent in each of these decisions—and in every policy decision—are trade-offs that inevitably create winners and losers. In the context of postsecondary education, that means access for some may be limited. Resources alone will not solve every policy dilemma, but Bloom, Canning, and Sevilla's (2002) assertion that "transforming a youthful population into a productive workforce requires investment in education at all levels" emphasizes that funding cannot be ignored.

Since resource limitations are a reality in even the best of economic times, some research efforts have tried to disaggregate the individual and public benefits of higher education and assign fiscal responsibility based on the benefit accrued to each. Disaggregating public from private benefits is a complicated endeavor. Adding to the difficulty is the intangible nature of some higher education benefits that Bowen's work described, such as personal growth and an individual's contribution to the public good. As such, many of the prominent commentaries on who should pay for higher education have tended to emphasize the monetary returns of higher education. In 1973, the Carnegie Commission on Higher Education (1973) concluded it reasonable if two-thirds of higher education costs were borne privately and one-third publicly. The commission's recommendation was based on multiple considerations, but distinctive among them was that college graduates retained approximately two-thirds of the additional income they received as a result of obtaining a degree.

While the precise proportions of fiscal responsibility are still far from clear, there is little question that higher education produces individual and public benefits. An individual earns more income in a lifetime because of higher education, and more absolute tax is paid to the government as a result of that increased income. Ideally, an individual develops his mind and learns to think critically, which results in more civic responsibility and less crime. The public and private benefits of higher education are intertwined and do not occur independently. Efforts to separate public and private benefits may be driven more by political necessity and resource constraint than a true representation of reality.

The perceptions of state leaders are integral to the discussion of higher education benefits. Policymakers believe that higher education leads to many public and private benefits in their states. In a recent national survey, state-level policymakers continually emphasized the link between higher education and state fiscal health. A number of legislators said that higher education is the engine of economic development for their states (Ruppert, 2001). This is because higher education carries the responsibility for creating a qualified workforce that will attract business and industry. A well-regarded research university can serve as an incentive for the location or relocation of high-tech industries. A recent report by the Milken Institute suggests this approach may have merit. Of the top 30 high-technology metropolitan areas, 29 are home to or within close proximity of a research university (DeVol, 1999). Such evidence is important to the future of higher education, because it is likely that institutions will have to increasingly emphasize their link to state or local economic activity to justify their existence.

Legislators across the country are undeniably concerned about the economic health of their states, but several of these same state leaders believe attending college goes beyond occupational preparation (Ruppert, 2001, p. 16). Legislative perceptions are aligned with Bowen's assertion that college attendance and completion leads to personal growth as well as increased civic responsibility. Legislators across the nation carry a common goal of increasing educational attainment among their populations (Ibid., p. i) because of the public and private benefits that result from such an improvement, and participation is a reasonable starting point to move toward that goal.

The Growing Case for Postsecondary Participation

The U.S. Census Bureau provides state-by-state statistics on the number of people participating in postsecondary education and the educational attainment level of the adult population. Individuals enrolled in education and training that counts as acceptable credit toward a degree are included in the census participation statistics. The census also tracks the number of individuals 25 and older who have earned a terminal degree and thus contribute to higher levels of educational attainment in the population.

Postsecondary participation is associated with many state benefits. A brief analysis of 2000 state-by-state decennial census data reveals that postsecondary participation is significantly related to various measures beneficial to individuals and society.[2] States that successfully enroll a large percentage of 18- to 24-year-olds in postsecondary education also tend to have

- High levels of educational attainment in the adult population,
- High degree completion,
- High percentage of people voting, and
- Low rates of poverty.

States that successfully enroll a large percentage of students 25 and older in postsecondary education tend to have

- High levels of educational attainment in the adult population,
- High median family income, and
- A low percentage of people with less than a high school credential.

Participation is statistically related to all of the benefits highlighted above. It would be incorrect to assume, based only on a statistical analysis, that participation is the sole contributor to each of these benefits. However, a statistically significant relationship between participation and a given benefit may indicate that participation leads to that benefit. For example, if a high percentage of 18- to 24-year-olds participate in higher education and completion rates are also strong, it is obvious that participation leads to completion. People need to participate before they can complete a degree. The positive relationship between high participation rates for students 25 and older and high median family income may be an indication that adult students returning to college eventually earn higher incomes.

It is possible that the statistical relationship between participation and a given benefit does not conclusively indicate whether participation leads to that benefit or the benefit preexisted and leads to more participation. It is also possible that participation and its associated benefits are simultaneously influencing each other. Educational attainment and 18- to 24-year-old participation is a good example. It is not clear whether high educational attainment in the population leads to high participation among the traditional student population or high participation leads to high educational attainment. Educated people tend to send their children to college. So a state ranking high on educational attainment may also rank high on participation because educated parents send their children to college. On the other hand, if participation leads to completion, then attainment is also strengthened. Traditional student participation and existing educational attainment levels likely influence one another. Educational attainment is also related to adult student participation. Many adults return to college on their own initiative, for personal growth or career advancement. Their participation and eventual success may strengthen educational attainment in their states.

The statistical relationship between postsecondary participation and educational attainment is particularly important to emphasize from a policy perspective. In Ruppert's two national surveys (Ruppert, 1996; Ruppert, 2001) of state legislators, policymakers expressed concern about postsecondary participation, and they are virtually unanimous in their goal of improving educational attainment in their states. It is only through participation that attainment is achieved. In addition to the correlation linking participation to educational attainment, other studies link greater levels of educational attainment to various measures of public and private benefit. The often cited benefit of higher education is that it leads to increased income for the individual, which produces increased income for the state. Figure 1.1 shows that this enduring perception is indeed correct.

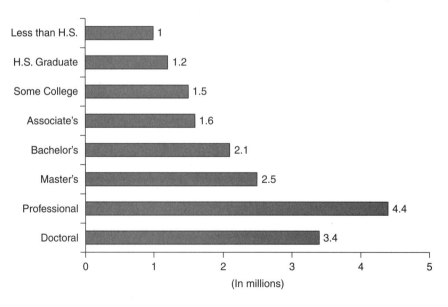

Figure 1.1 Comparison of lifetime earnings and educational attainment. (*Source: U.S. Census Bureau, Current Population Survey, March 2000.*)

The message of Figure 1.1 is that higher levels of educational attainment produce higher lifetime earnings. The only exception to this rule is at the highest level of attainment. In general, individuals who obtain a professional degree earn more than those who obtain a doctoral degree. Professional degree recipients include MBAs and lawyers, while doctoral recipients are from every discipline and often teach in colleges and universities.

The gap in lifetime earnings between those who have a college degree and those who do not has been growing since 1980. Perna (2003) reports that the earnings premium associated with attaining at least a bachelor's degree rather than a high school diploma nearly tripled between 1980 and 1999 for men and almost doubled for women during this same time period. There are indications that the earnings premium associated with additional education beyond high school will only grow over time. For example, most new jobs added by today's economy are being filled by workers with at least some postsecondary education (Vernez, Krop, & Rydell, 1999). The census also reports that some college is better than no college. Those who attend college without obtaining a bachelor's degree earn more than those who terminate their education with a high school credential. An associate's degree increases lifetime earnings still more, but educational attainment up to and after the bachelor's degree shows dramatic differences compared to anything less than a bachelor's degree. A study by Vernez, Krop, and Rydell (1999) not only confirms that higher levels of educational attainment lead to higher income but, in turn, produce higher public revenues through federal and state taxes (pp. 26–30).

Educational attainment also produces benefits that go beyond improved fiscal outcomes for individuals and the state. In a recent report, McGuinness and Jones (2003) report that states with low levels of educational attainment also rank low on measures of health of the population, child well-being, and civic participation (in terms of voting). A deeper look at just one of these measures is even more revealing. For example, the gauge for state health in the McGuinness and Jones (2003) study is provided by the United Health Foundation (United Health Foundation, 2002). A panel of public health scholars periodically reviews and weighs the factors that the organization uses to assess the health of a state's population. Examples of the factors used to assess health include prevalence of smoking, violent crimes, poverty, and incidence of preventable diseases. Each of these factors is important to the states and the individuals living in the states. Low educational attainment, according to McGuinness and Jones, leads to lower levels of health for a state's population. A summary interpretation is that poorly educated states fare poorly across various statistics that speak to quality of life.

If low educational attainment corresponds to lower quality of life in a state, it follows that high educational attainment levels correspond to improved performance on quality-of-life measures. The research by Vernez, Krop and Rydell (1999) validates this corollary assumption. These authors find that education leads to reduced crime, improved social cohesion, technological innovation, and intergenerational benefits (p. 13). There are also significant savings in public program costs as educational attainment rises (p. 24). In the end, the value of improving state postsecondary participation is that it is the starting point to improve educational attainment, which in turn produces public and private benefits.

States and nations that improve the educational attainment level of their populations will reap the rewards that accompany their efforts. Economist Lester Thurow (2000) differentiates between public investment and public consumption, both of which require taxpayer monies. Education is a form of public investment. Singapore is an example of a country that has focused on postsecondary education and received many benefits as a result. Singapore invested more money in education than any society in the world to attract technology and push its income per capita to internationally competitive levels (p. 231).

The public and private benefits associated with higher education are certainly maximized if those who participate eventually complete a degree. Gladieux (2002) outlines the importance of not stopping at entry and the need to help students through to completion. The RAND study by Vernez, Krop, and Rydell (1999) demonstrates that some college is better than no college, but increased levels of postsecondary attainment correspond to increased public and private benefits. There are certainly states that must do more to see their students through to completion, but Martinez, Farias, and Arellano's (2002) research does indicate that for the states in general, higher participation leads to higher completion rates. Postsecondary participation, then, can legitimately be thought of as the starting point for the production of public and private benefits.

CHAPTER 2

The Current State of Postsecondary Participation

A profile of the current state of postsecondary participation provides a basis for comparison with future demand. Several authorities in the area of planning (Goodstein & Burke, 1995; Mintzberg, 1994; Senge, 1990) emphasize that effective change requires efforts to compare current conditions with future scenarios. A systematic effort to reach the desired future scenario is best accomplished through planning (Goodstein & Burke, 1995) and policymaking.

This chapter serves as the starting point for state higher education planning efforts by providing current state-by-state postsecondary statistics. Chapter 3 provides a future enrollment scenario for the Year 2015 for all 50 states, assuming that states maintain their current participation rates in the future. Chapter 4 provides additional future enrollment scenarios, assuming that states will improve their participation rates. Current postsecondary participation can be compared against the various future enrollment scenarios to examine the extent and range of the changes that policymakers can expect in the future.

The Current Picture of Postsecondary Participation

The U.S. Census Bureau recently released postsecondary participation by age for every state in the country for the Year 2000. Based on the Census 2000 questionnaire, postsecondary participation means a person residing in the state attended a public or private degree-granting college or university at any time since February 2000.[3] The total number of students participating in postsecondary education for all states

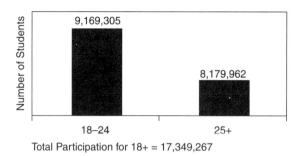

Figure 2.1 National postsecondary participation by age group. (*Source: U.S. Census, 2002. Calculated from detailed state tables for 2000, Table PCT 24.*)

equals postsecondary participation for the nation. Figure 2.1 shows national postsecondary participation for two age groups in the 18 and older population.

The combined total of persons 18 and older (18+) participating in postsecondary education in 2000 was 17,349,267, as shown in Figure 2.1. This combined total represents 18- to 24-year-olds plus students 25 and older (25+). Postsecondary participation totals for the 50 states, by age group, are shown in the first two columns of Appendix A.

The census postsecondary participation statistics include graduate and undergraduate students who attended either public or private two- or four-year degree-granting institutions. Figure 2.1 therefore represents a comprehensive picture of national postsecondary participation as obtained by Census 2000 household survey results.

The percentage of a state's population participating in postsecondary education is known as its participation rate. Participation rates are particularly important to track because they are a barometer of higher education access. Absolute enrollment numbers can be deceiving if they are not considered relative to a state's population. For example, due to population growth, a state's absolute enrollment could increase even though it is actually providing access to a smaller proportion of the population. Current participation rates can be calculated from the following decennial census data sets:

- The number of students in postsecondary education in the two age groups of interest: 18- to 24-year-olds and 25 and older; and
- The total number of people in the general population for each age group.

Table 2.1 National Postsecondary Participation Statistics

Age Group	Total Number of Students	Total Age Group Population	Participation Rate (students/population)
18–24	9,169,305	26,994,318	34.0%
25+	8,179,962	181,827,104	4.5%
18+ (total)	17,349,267	208,821,22	8.3%

(*Source:* U.S. Census, 2002. Calculated from detailed state tables for 2000, Table PCT 24.)

The participation rate is the number of students in postsecondary education divided by the total population. Participation rates can be calculated for the two age groups of interest, as shown below.

Participation rate (18–24) = Number of students (18- to 24-year-olds)/Total number of 18- to 24-year-olds in the general population

Participation rate (25+) = Number of students (25+)/Total number of people 25 and older in the general population

Table 2.1 shows the national totals, by age group, for: (1) the number of students, (2) the total population, and (3) the participation rate. The last row in the table is the combined total for 18- to 24-year-olds and those 25 and older. Although the focus is primarily on these two age groups, the combined total (18+) is provided in the table for completeness. Current participation and population figures and participation rates, by age group, for every state and the nation are shown in Appendix A.

The national number of students by age group is the sum of all students in that age group for all 50 states. It is important to note that at the state level the census counts students not by state of origin but where they are attending college. The census has enumerated students this way since 1950, so enrollments calculated by state from other sources may yield differences depending on assumptions and methodology. The national population by age group is the sum of all people in that age group (those participating and not participating in postsecondary education) for all 50 states.

Over one-third of the 18- to 24-year-old population participates in postsecondary education in the country. Students in this age range account for 52.9 percent of the over 17 million people 18 and older who reported to the census that they participate in some form of postsecondary education. Of the general population 25 and older, 4.5 percent participate in some form of postsecondary education. The number of students 25 and older participating in postsecondary education has been increasing steadily in the United States. In states such as Maryland and Nevada, the adult student population is already in the majority.[4] All else equal, states expecting growth in the 25 and older population should also expect an increase in enrollment demand from this age group.

Population by Age

Population by age group is commonly referred to as age structure. A study by Bloom, Canning, and Sevilla (2002) outlined the importance of age structure on a country's economic development. The authors also concluded that investment in education is linked to age structure and merits policy attention. Based on these findings, state higher education policy should be sensitive to population increases in the college-eligible population to maximize economic potential.

Age structure in the United States is relatively predictable and readily available from the census. These features make it an ideal variable to use for analysis and planning purposes, for projecting enrollments, or for comparison with other access-related statistics. Figure 2.2 shows the proportion of 18- to 24-year-olds and people 25 and older in the United States. These statistics are for the entire 18 and older population, both those enrolled in postsecondary education and those not enrolled. The 2000 age group proportions for each state are shown in the first two columns of Appendix B.

The proportion of 18- to 24-year-olds and people 25 and older varies across the states. From a policy perspective, the presence of large

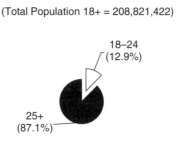

Figure 2.2   Age group proportions for the nation, 18 and older. (*Source: U.S. Census, 2002. Calculated from detailed state tables for 2000, Table PCT 24.*)

subpopulations often increases the level of state services provided to those subpopulations. A large proportion of elementary school children or elderly citizens might logically require states to focus resources on K–12 or senior services. Do states behave in this manner with respect to higher education? Do states with a high proportion of 18- to 24-year-olds provide more postsecondary opportunities and services for this population? On the other hand, should participation rates in such states be lower than average, given the resource constraints and difficulty of providing for such a high proportion of 18- to 24-year-olds? Consider the profiles for the following two states:

> Profile 1: Florida's 18- to 24-year-old participation rate is 31.7 percent, which is below the national average participation rate of 34.0 percent. The proportion of 18- to 24-year-olds in the 18 and older population is 10.7 percent, which is well below the national average of 12.9 percent.
>
> Profile 2: Illinois's 18- to 24-year-old participation rate is 34.8 percent, which is slightly above the national average participation rate of 34.0 percent. The proportion of 18- to 24-year-olds in the 18 and older population is 13.1 percent, which is also above the national average of 12.9 percent.

The two profiles raise some important issues. Are the participation rates for Florida and Illinois reasonable, given the relative sizes of their 18- to 24-year-old populations? Should we expect Illinois to have a higher participation rate than Florida, and if so, how high should it be? Should Florida's participation rate be higher, based on the smaller proportion of 18- to 24-year-olds in its population? It is possible to answer these questions by combining age group proportions and participation rates into one indicator.

When participation rates are examined relative to age group proportions, the variation across age structure is taken into account. States then have a tool to validly compare participation rates even though their age structures may differ. Policymakers can use this tool to ask what their states' participation rates should be, given their states' age structures. Three important policy-related questions arise when age structure and participation rates are considered concurrently:

1. Is a state's participation rate for each age group reasonable, given the state's population represented by that age group?
2. What level of participation for each age group should a state expect, given the state's population represented by that age group?

3. After controlling for age group proportions in the 18 and older population, do the states show wide differences on other factors related to state context?

The three policy questions will guide the analysis for the rest of the chapter. Before the questions can be fully answered, a brief introduction to financial ratio analysis is necessary. Financial ratio analysis combines two statistics and can be used to compare participation rates across states, relative to age structure.

Applying Financial Ratio Analysis to Postsecondary Participation

Financial ratio analysis has long been a common practice in the business arena (Foster, 1986). Financial ratio analysis combines two numbers into a ratio, effectively standardizing one number relative to the other. The two measures used in a ratio should be meaningfully related. A common ratio in private industry, for example, is return on assets. Return on assets is income divided by assets (net income/total assets). The return on assets ratio measures the efficiency with which total assets are employed within an organization. This ratio and the two measures that comprise it are meaningfully related since private organizations are interested in understanding how much income they are generating from their existing assets.

The concept of financial ratio analysis can be applied to state higher education policy analysis to produce insights about higher education access. Age structure, specifically age group proportions, impacts how many students participate today and how many will demand access in the future. The use of age group proportions and participation rates are therefore meaningfully linked and can be combined into a single ratio. Using this ratio, states can assess their participation rates given the age group proportions that comprise their populations. This assessment can then be compared with other states to answer the first policy question previously stated: Is a state's participation rate for each age group reasonable, given the state's population represented by that age group?

The second policy question asks what participation rates should states expect, given the state's population represented by that age group. Expected participation rates can only be calculated if the states have a basis for comparison. A national ratio comprised of the national participation rate and the national age group proportion (for each age group) can be calculated to serve this purpose. The national comparison ratio can be compared to an individual state's comparison ratio to calculate an expected participation rate for the state. An example of this calculation will be shown in the next section.

Once an expected participation rate is calculated, it is possible to answer the second policy question. A significant difference between the expected and actual participation rate for a given state suggests that factors other than age structure possibly may be influencing postsecondary participation. More research may point to some of these factors, which would answer the third policy question: After controlling for age group proportions in the 18 and older population, do the states show wide differences on other factors related to state context?

State participation rate comparisons provide information about higher education access. State participation rate comparisons that account for state demographic differences provide additional insight that can help answer important policy questions. The ratios in this chapter combine participation rates and age group proportions into one measure using census data for the Year 2000. These ratios enhance comparisons of state higher education access and are hereafter referred to as comparison ratios. The definitions for the two comparison ratios used for the remainder of the chapter are shown below:

Comparison ratio (18–24) = Participation rate (18–24)/Proportion of 18- to 24-year-olds in the 18 and older general population

Comparison ratio (25+) = Participation rate (25+)/Proportion of 25+ in the 18 and older general population

Table 2.2 provides participation rates by age group, age group proportions, and comparison ratios for the nation and six select states. The six states were not chosen at random. The states with the highest 18- to 24-year-old and 25+ participation rates in the country (Rhode Island and California, respectively) are represented in the table. Also represented are the states with the lowest 18- to 24-year-old and 25+ participation rates in the country (Alaska and West Virginia, respectively). Utah is included in the analysis because it has the highest proportion of 18- to 24-year-olds in the 18 and older population in the country and the lowest proportion of people 25 and older. Connecticut has the lowest proportion of 18- to 24-year-olds in the 18 and older population in the country and the highest proportion of people 25 and older.

The comparison ratios for each state are in the last column of the table. Appendix B contains the 2000 comparison ratios for the 50 states and the nation. Each state's participation rates and the proportion of 18- to 24-year-olds and those 25 and older affect the value of the

Table 2.2 Sample of State Postsecondary Participation Statistics

	Participation Rate (%)		Proportion of 18 and Over Population (%)		Comparison Ratio: Rate/Proportion	
	18–24	25+	18–24	25+	18–24	25+
United States	34.0	4.5	12.9	87.1	2.64	.052
Rhode Island	47.7*	4.8	13.3	86.7	3.59	.055
Utah	36.6	5.8	21.0*	79.0**	1.74	.073
California	35.4	6.4*	13.6	86.4	2.60	.074
Alaska	19.2**	5.6	13.0	87.0	1.48	.064
West Virginia	33.2	2.8**	12.3	87.7	2.70	.032
Connecticut	38.3	4.4	10.5**	89.5*	3.65	.049

*Highest rank among the 50 states in this category.
**Lowest rank among the 50 states in this category.

comparison ratio. The national comparison ratio for 18- to 24-year-olds is 2.64 (34.0%/12.9%). The national comparison ratio for this age group can be used to assess whether each state's participation rate is at the expected level, given the proportion of 18- to 24-year-olds in the 18 and older population. States with a comparison ratio above 2.64 are producing higher participation rates for this age group than would be expected, given the proportion of 18- to 24-year-olds in the 18 and older population. States with a comparison ratio below 2.64 are producing lower participation rates for this age group than would be expected, given the proportion of 18- to 24-year-olds in the 18 and older population.

The national comparison ratio for the 25+ age group is .052 (4.5%/87.1%). The national comparison ratio for this age group can be used to assess whether each state's participation rate is at the expected level, given the proportion of people 25 and older in the 18 and older population. States with a comparison ratio above .052 are producing higher participation rates for this age group than would be expected, given the proportion of the people 25 and older in the 18 and older population. States with a comparison ratio below .052 are producing lower participation rates for this age group than would be expected, given the proportion of the people 25 and older in the 18 and older population.

Table 2.2 now serves as a guide to answer the three policy questions from earlier in the chapter, with the comparison ratio as the focus. Each age group will be analyzed separately, and the policy questions will be explored in sequence, using the information from the table.

18- to 24-Year-Olds

Is a given state's participation rate for 18- to 24-year-olds reasonable, given the proportion of the state's population represented by this age group?

The current national participation rate for 18- to 24-year-olds is 34.0 percent, meaning that over one-third of 18- to 24-year-olds in the United States participate in some form of postsecondary education. The two eastern states in Table 2.2, Connecticut and Rhode Island, have participation rates well above the national average. Rhode Island's 47.7 percent rate leads the nation. California and Utah have slightly higher than average participation rates for this age group, while Alaska and West Virginia are below the national average.

The state participation rate for 18- to 24-year-olds gives policymakers one measure of postsecondary access. The comparison ratio can be used to determine whether each state's participation rate is acceptable given the proportion of the 18- to 24-year-olds in the 18 and older population.

The national comparison ratio for 18- to 24-year-olds is 2.64. Rhode Island, Connecticut, and West Virginia each have comparison ratios above the national average for this age group. This means that each of these states is producing a participation rate beyond what would be expected. For example, West Virginia has a smaller proportion of 18- to 24-year-olds in its 18 and older population than the national average, yet its participation rate is close to the national participation rate. Using only the participation rate, West Virginia appears to lag behind the nation in terms of providing access to its 18- to 24-year-old population, but the state's comparison ratio is higher than the national comparison ratio. This means that West Virginia's participation rate is actually better than expected, given the proportion of 18- to 24-year-olds in the 18 and older population.

The national comparison ratio sets a standard and defines what participation rate is appropriate given the proportion of 18- to 24-year-olds in the 18 and older population. The national comparison ratio is an average because it is calculated from data for all 50 states, so it offers a logical standard for comparison. Those states with lower than average participation rates must have lower than average proportions of 18- to

24-year-olds to equal the national comparison ratio. Those states with higher than average proportions of 18- to 24-year-olds must have higher than average participation rates to equal the national comparison ratio.

California and Utah have above average participation rates but below average comparison ratios. Alaska's participation rate for 18- to 24-year-olds is well below the national average, as is its comparison ratio. The comparison ratio for these three states indicates that participation rates for 18- to 24-year-olds should be higher, given the proportion of 18- to 24-year-olds in the 18 and older population. California's higher than average proportion of 18- to 24-year-olds lowers the state's comparison ratio. Still, California's participation rate and comparison ratio for this age group are very close to the national averages. Alaska and Utah have particularly low comparison ratios, indicating that differences in state policy or a state contextual factor other than age structure may be influencing performance. The issue of state context will be considered after the expected participation rates are calculated for the three states with lower than average comparison ratios.

What level of participation for the 18- to 24-age group should a state expect, given the state's population represented by that age group?

States can figure out their expected participation rates by age group by looking at the national comparison ratio. If a state wishes to obtain a comparison ratio equal to the national average, then either the participation rate or the proportion of 18- to 24-year-olds in the 18 and older population must change. Age group proportions are not easily changed by state policy and are part of a state's context. Since the age group proportion is considered a state contextual factor, it is the participation rate that is most amenable to policy influence. The expected participation rate that would result in a state comparison rate equal to the national comparison ratio is given by the following calculation:

Expected participation rate (18–24) = Proportion of 18- to 24-year-olds in the 18 and older population * National comparison ratio for 18- to 24-year-olds

Given the proportion of 18- to 24-year-olds in Alaska, California, and Utah, the participation rates for these states would have to increase to achieve comparison ratios equal to the national average.

- Alaska's expected participation rate = 34.3 percent (2.64 * 13.0%)
  Alaska's current participation rate = 19.2 percent
- California's expected participation rate = 35.9 percent (2.64 * 13.6%)
  California's current participation rate = 35.4 percent

- Utah's expected participation rate = 55.4 percent (2.64 * 21.0%)
- Utah's current participation rate = 36.6 percent

If the three states obtained their expected participation rates, each would provide the expected level of access to 18- to 24-year-olds given the proportion of this age group in the 18 and older population. California's expected participation rate of 35.9 percent is very close to its current participation rate of 35.4 percent. Alaska and Utah would have to make enormous gains just to reach their expected participation rates. Large disparities between actual and expected participation rates may indicate prominent variations in state policies or state contextual factors other than age structure. State policies change frequently and are difficult to document systematically. For this reason, the last policy question focuses on state contextual factors—other than age structure—that may be causing the large disparities.

After controlling for age group proportions in the 18 and older population, do the states show wide differences on other factors related to state context?

From a macro perspective, state participation is influenced by state policy and state contextual factors. State contextual factors include demographic, geographic, historic, social, and economic factors. Most of these factors are not easily or immediately controlled by institutions or the state. Of all the possible state contextual factors that affect participation, the comparison ratio controls for one demographic factor across the states—the age group proportions of 18- to 24-year-olds and those 25 and older. The third policy question is meant to highlight additional state contextual factors that may be influencing the difference between actual and expected participation rates.

State contextual differences can provide a backdrop for policy discussions but should not be used as the sole explanation for performance across the range of participation statistics. State context does not fully explain higher education performance and should not be used as a singular rationalization for lower or higher performance results (Martinez, Farias, & Arellano, 2002; NCPPHE, 2000; Cunningham & Wellman, 2001). In addition, state-by-state comparisons would be meaningless if state contextual differences alone explained a state's participation results.

Policymakers have shown an interest in comparing their states across different measures of higher education performance and looking at the best practices of other states (Ruppert, 1996), because they know that policy matters. At the same time, most policymakers consider their states unique. It is for this reason that they are also interested in context, and the consideration of context may help them make state comparisons that they consider meaningful. It is to that end that contextual differences among the states in Table 2.2 are now highlighted against participation.

Higher Than Expected Performance

Connecticut and Rhode Island produce impressive participation results for their 18- to 24-year-old populations. Both states have relatively small populations and are situated in the East, where students have geographic accessibility to public and private institutions. Connecticut and Rhode Island also attract students from other states. The small populations in both states mean that one college participant has a larger impact on participation rates than would be true if that participant attended college in a state with a very large population base.

Connecticut and Rhode Island are above the national average for state contextual measures such as median family income and educational attainment levels of their adult populations. Connecticut, in particular, performs extremely well on these measures. In Connecticut, the 2000 median family income of $65,521 was well above the national average of $49,242.[5] Finally, Connecticut and Rhode Island have relatively homogenous populations compared to other states.[6] In general, states with proportionately small minority populations do not experience the range of needs and challenges that arise in states with populations that are more ethnically and racially diverse. The combination of high incomes and homogeneous populations in Connecticut and Rhode Island suggests that these two states may not face some of the educational challenges that more diverse states face.

Lower Than Expected Performance

Although Utah has a higher than average participation rate for 18- to 24-year-olds, the state's comparison ratio is well below the national average. Utah has the highest concentration of 18- to 24-year-olds in its 18 and older population compared to any other state, but its low comparison ratio indicates a lower than expected participation rate. In its Measuring Up 2000 higher education report card, the National Center for Public Policy and Higher Education (NCPPHE) noted that its measurement of higher education completion in the state of Utah may have been lower than actual performance since many Mormon students leave colleges and universities for two years to fulfill a service mission and then return to complete a degree (NCPPHE, 2000). The NCPPHE clearly felt that the religious culture of the state was affecting Utah's performance on higher education completion.

Utah's current participation rate of 36.6 percent is below its expected rate of 55.4 percent, given the current proportion of 18- to 24-year-olds in the 18 and older population. The religious culture of the state may be influencing participation rates for 18- to 24-year-olds for one of the following reasons: (1) those who fulfill a two-year service mission return to the state but do not enroll in postsecondary education, or (2) those who fulfill a two-year service mission return to the state and are enrolled in postsecondary education past the age of 24. If the latter assumption is true, then Utah's participation statistics for the 25 and older population should be favorable relative to the nation. Table 2.2 in fact shows that Utah's participation rate and comparison ratio for the 25+ age group are above the national averages for these two statistics. It is conceivable that the religious culture in Utah is contributing to the results the state achieves on the various participation statistics in Table 2.2.

Alaska is also well below the national average in terms of its 18- to 24-year-old participation rate and comparison ratio. Alaska's geographical location may be influencing participation results because it is so distant from other states. The state does not attract a significant number of out-of-state college students. Perhaps more importantly, Alaska has not been successful convincing first-time freshmen to attend college in the state. The number of freshmen leaving Alaska to attend college in other states is virtually equal to those who attend college in the state (NCES, 2001a).

25 and Older

Is a given state's participation rate for those 25 and older reasonable, given the proportion of the state's population represented by this age group?

Nationally, 4.5 percent of people 25 and older participate in some form of postsecondary education. California's 6.4 percent participation rate for people 25 and older easily leads the nation. The two other western states in Table 2.2, Utah and Alaska, also have relatively high participation rates for this age group. Rhode Island's 25+ participation rate is also slightly above the national average. West Virginia and Connecticut have lower than average participation rates for this age group.

The national comparison ratio for the 25+ age group is .052. All four states that have a higher than average participation rate for this age group also have a higher than average comparison ratio. This indicates that Alaska, California, Rhode Island, and Utah all produce higher than expected participation rates for the 25+ age group, given the proportion of people 25 and older in the 18 and older population.

West Virginia and Connecticut have higher than average proportions of people 25 and older and lower than average participation rates for the 25+ group. West Virginia's 2.8 percent participation rate is the lowest in the nation. The lower than average comparison ratios for these states indicate lower than expected participation rates. West Virginia's .032 comparison ratio is particularly low. These initial results suggest that Connecticut and West Virginia are not meeting the postsecondary needs of their 25 and older populations, as compared to other states in the nation. The additional policy questions are helpful to determine whether there are other factors that help explain the performance of these two states.

What level of participation for the 25+ age group should a state expect, given the state's population represented by that age group?

Given the proportion of people 25 and older in Connecticut and West Virginia, the participation rates for these states would have to increase to achieve comparison ratios equal to the national average.

- Connecticut's expected participation rate = 4.7 percent (.052 * 89.5%)

  Connecticut's current participation rate = 4.4 percent

- West Virginia's expected participation rate = 4.6 percent (.052 * 87.7%)

  West Virginia's current participation rate = 2.8 percent

If the two states obtained their expected participation rates, each would provide the expected level of access to those 25 and older, given the representation of this age group in the 18 and older population. Given the higher than average proportions of people 25 and older in Connecticut and West Virginia, each state's expected participation rate is higher than the national average of 4.5 percent. Connecticut would have to make modest gains in its 25+ participation rate to reach expected levels. The improvement required of West Virginia is so great that it seems reasonable to look at whether any state contextual factors are contributing to the state's low performance.

After controlling for age group proportions in the 18 and older population, do the states show wide differences on other factors related to state context?

Higher Than Expected Performance

California's nation leading participation performance for the 25+ age group may be as much a product of its 1960s Master Plan design as any state contextual factors. The California Community College sector is well developed and has played an important role in the state's history. In general, students at community colleges tend to be older than those at four-year institutions, so California appears to have an infrastructure in place to serve the 25 and older population. States such as New Mexico, Arizona, and Washington have higher than average comparison ratios for the 25+ population (Appendix B), and all of these states also have well-developed community college systems.

Utah has a small proportion of people 25 and older, and a high concentration of those people participate in postsecondary participation. Utah's community college system is not particularly strong in terms of the proportion of students it enrolls relative to total postsecondary enrollment for the state. Unlike California, Utah's participation results for the 25 and older population cannot be explained by a well-developed community college system. The role of religious culture may be contributing to the strong participation statistics for the 25 and older population in the state. The postsecondary enrollment delays associated with service missions are likely contributing to the state's strong performance on participation statistics for the 25 and older population.

Lower Than Expected Performance

West Virginia's participation statistics for the 25 and older population are below the national averages. The state context in West Virginia presents several educational challenges. According to state-by-state 2000 decennial census, West Virginia has the lowest percentage of college graduates (including associates, bachelors, graduate, and professional combined) of any state and ranks near the top in terms of the percentage of its adult population without a high school diploma.[7] The state's poverty rate is high and its median family income is low. In addition to these challenges, a very small percentage of postsecondary enrollments in the state are in the two-year sector. This would indicate that a common avenue for postsecondary participation for people 25 and older is not as available in West Virginia as might be true in other states. A strong two-year sector is important for a population that lags in terms of educational attainment and the percentage of people without a high school diploma. The West Virginia legislature did take steps in 2000 to ensure the availability of community college services in each region.[8] Whether the legislative changes improve participation rates remains to be seen.

Like West Virginia, Connecticut's participation statistics for the 25 and older population are slightly below the national averages. In the case of Connecticut, it is notable that the educational attainment levels for the 25 and older population are among the highest in the nation. It is very likely that a larger percentage of the 25 and older population in Connecticut is not enrolled in some form of postsecondary education because so many of these individuals already have a college degree and so have little need to participate.

Conclusion

Postsecondary participation is an important indicator of future public and private benefits. Postsecondary participation today creates the necessary human capital to sustain or develop state economic progress tomorrow. The individual benefits of higher education include personal, social, and cultural satisfaction. While current participation rates provide one measure of a state's commitment to its citizens, the nature of each state's demographics further informs whether those participation rates are competitive relative to the nation and other states. Any statistic related to current postsecondary participation is really just a starting point to help states expand access. Such statistics give states an idea of where they are so that they can plan to reach their goals more fully informed of the work that lies ahead.

CHAPTER 3

The Future State of Postsecondary Participation

Postsecondary participation rates from Chapter 2 are used in this chapter to project future enrollment demand for 2015. A comparison of current and future enrollments provides an indication of how much access will have to expand in the future. The enrollment projections in this chapter assume that states maintain their current participation rates in the future—there are no increases or decreases in participation rates. All else equal, states would have to maintain their current levels of higher education services to maintain participation rates in the future. In turn, this would require that states provide the investment necessary to maintain higher education services.

Participation rates, service levels, and funding amounts will affect access in the future. Assumptions must be made about each of these factors to quantify their affect on future enrollment demand. Assumptions are not always easy to predict, but those that can be reasonably predicted can be integrated into future enrollment projections. Some additional factors that will influence future enrollment demand include

- Changes in high school graduation rates, changes in dropout rates, or changes in both graduation and dropout rates
- Changes in the number of high school graduates
- Improvements in academic performance among high school students
- Improvements in adult education
- Advances/changes in technology and curriculum delivery

- Effective recruitment strategies by institutions or states
- Changes in student aid or institutional financing policies
- Tax incentives
- Shifts and changes in the size and composition of the 18 and older population

Many of the factors listed above will influence future demand, but they are highly unpredictable or difficult to quantify. State policy actions, institutional behaviors, and economic trends are extremely difficult to predict and quantify, though each will influence access. Even today, the policy tools states use to improve high school graduation rates or stimulate interest in adult education are highly diffuse and nonstandardized across states. Similarly, effective recruitment strategies by institutions (and sometimes states) are often localized and confined to one state if not one region of one state. The policy tools and recruitment strategies of the future are not yet known, and they are likely to remain diffuse and nonstandardized. There is no systematic way to account for the influence these factors will have on future enrollment demand across the states.

Technology and access are often discussed in tandem. The impact of technological innovation on higher education access has been the subject of much speculation (Heller, 2001a; Privateer, 1999). Though there is little doubt that technology affects access, establishing its effect remains elusive and difficult to document. This will continue to be the case, as the impact of any transforming technology though revolutionary can take years or even decades to manifest itself in a tangible way (Taylor, 1996). The wide variation in technology acceptance, adoption, and implementation makes it an unstable source for predicting future enrollments.

Even if technology appears to be poised for use in higher education, its implementation is unpredictable. One survey found consistent enthusiasm among state policymakers for plans to invest in state technology infrastructure as a means to address such issues as higher education efficiency and access (Ruppert, 1996). In another survey five years later, the tone from many of these same policymakers was much less optimistic. Many of the legislators from the first survey indicated in the second survey that the implementation of technology was more complicated than originally thought. Several states were confronting issues related to upfront investment costs and quality (Ruppert, 2001). Startup costs associated with technological solutions are particularly problematic for states, as such investment often bumps up against spending constraints or competing needs.

The size and composition of the 18 and older population is another factor that influences access. The 18 and older population by age group served an important role in Chapter 2. Age group populations were used to construct participation rates and help answer policy-relevant questions. Future age group projections will be used in a similar manner in this chapter. Census provides state-by-state demographic projections for the age groups of interest. These projections are easily accessible and among the most credible available.

Future enrollment projections in this chapter rely on demographic projections for 2015. The census also provides detailed state projections for 2010, 2020, and 2025. The 2015 projections are the focal point because 2015 is far enough into the future to encourage forward thinking and close enough to the present that it includes the majority of today's adults and children. The construction of the enrollment projections is a two-step process.

1. Outline the 2015 projected size of the two age groups of interest, for the nation and the states; and
2. Multiply each age group's 2015 population by its status quo participation rate, by state, to get the projected enrollment demand by age group.

The analyses in steps 3 and 4 below help identify the differences among the states in meeting future access needs.

3. For each state, compare 2000 enrollment with the projected enrollment for 2015 to obtain the change in enrollment between 2000 and 2015; and
4. Demonstrate how projected shifts in the age group proportions affect the state comparison ratios derived in Chapter 2.

The 2015 projected enrollment by age group and state uses the 2015 population for each age group and multiplies it by the 2000 age group participation rate. This method of projection assumes that 2000 participation rates will be maintained in 2015. This establishes what is called a Baseline scenario for future enrollment. The effect of future demographic changes on future enrollment demand is easily discerned since the Baseline scenario assumes status quo participation rates but changing age group populations.

State budget projections typically include a Baseline scenario. Baseline state budget projections commonly apply current government policies to predicted future changes in the environment in order to measure the fiscal consequences of continuing those policies (Hovey, 1999, p. 1). Similarly, the Baseline scenario in this chapter applies current participation rates to predicted demographic changes to measure the impact of age structure on future enrollment. Chapter 4 will deviate from these status quo assumptions and ask the question, "If states improved their current participation rates in the future, what would enrollment demand look like in 2015?"

2015 Age Group Populations

The states vary in terms of the current size and proportion of 18- to 24-year-olds and those 25 and older. Onto 2015, these two age groups will grow at different rates in different states. In some states, both age groups will increase in absolute terms, but each will grow at a different rate. This will result in shifts in the proportions each age group accounts for in the 18 and older population. The 25 and older population will grow faster than the 18- to 24-year-old population in some states, while the opposite will be true for others. Finally, some states will look very similar in 2015 as they did in 2000. For example, many midwestern states will experience little population growth, and the proportional representation of the two age groups will remain virtually unchanged.

Table 3.1 shows the 2000 and 2015 populations for a select group of states for three age groups: 18- to 24-year-olds, 25 and older (25+), and 18 and older (18+). The 2000 statistics are actual population figures from the decennial census, and the 2015 population statistics are census projections. The 18+ category is the sum of both age groups.

There are 10 states under each age group in Table 3.1. The first five states in each age group show the highest percentage population growth between 2000 and 2015. The last five states in each age group show the lowest percentage population changes between 2000 and 2015. For some states with the lowest age group population changes, the 2015 projected age group total is less than the 2000 age group total. It is possible for the same state to appear in more than one age group category in Table 3.1. Appendix C contains 2015 age population statistics for all 50 states.

Nationally, the 18 and older population is projected to grow to over 235 million people by 2015, up from 181.8 million in 2000. The 18- to 24-year-old population will only account for 30.5 million of the total, primarily since this age group spans a smaller number of ages. However, the impact of this age group is important to future postsecondary projections since it captures the traditional student population.

Table 3.1 Age Group Population Comparisons: 2000 and 2015

18- to 24-Year-Olds	2000	2015	Percentage Change
Alaska	56,869	87,809	54.4%
California	3,351,285	4,718,293	40.8%
Hawaii	114,735	156,012	36.0%
Maryland	447,472	564,931	26.2%
New Mexico	176,677	220,384	24.7%
Kentucky	401,531	384,071	−4.3%
Arkansas	262,142	249,447	−4.8%
Mississippi	312,737	294,203	−5.9%
Iowa	298,134	267,436	−10.3%
West Virginia	172,988	153,473	−11.3%
25+			
Idaho	787,505	1,066,044	35.4%
Wyoming	315,663	422,277	33.8%
Utah	1,197,892	1,558,634	30.1%
New Mexico	1,134,801	1,451,741	27.9%
Montana	586,621	741,511	26.4%
Pennsylvania	8,266,284	8,593,689	4.0%
Massachusetts	4,273,275	4,428,433	3.6%
Rhode Island	694,573	714,360	2.8%
Michigan	6,415,941	6,590,137	2.7%
New York	12,542,536	12,379,977	−1.3%
Total (18+)			
Wyoming	365,685	480,665	31.4%
Idaho	925,822	1,211,483	30.9%
New Mexico	1,311,478	1,672,125	27.5%
Alaska	436,425	549,185	25.8%
Hawaii	917,212	1,144,528	24.8%

(continued)

Table 3.1 Continued			
Total (18+)	2000	2015	Percentage Change
Illinois	9,180,064	9,624,092	4.8%
Pennsylvania	9,362,066	9,710,551	3.7%
Rhode Island	800,810	822,516	2.7%
Michigan	7,345,849	7,526,244	2.5%
New York	14,302,266	14,338,458	0.3%

(*Source:* U.S. Census 2015 projections obtained in 2002 (www.census.gov). Age group populations for 2000 from Table PCT 24, decennial census.)

Several western states will experience large population increases, but the growth will occur in different age groups. The 18- to 24-year-old population in Alaska, California, Hawaii, and New Mexico will increase in 2015. The large percentage increases in Alaska, Hawaii, and New Mexico are largely because these states have smaller population bases than many other states. In these states, a small population increase in number translates into a larger percentage increase than would be true for a larger state. All five states at the bottom of the 18- to 24-year-old category in Table 3.1 will see their population for this age group decrease. Four of the five states are situated in the South.

All five states that are projected to see the largest percentage increases in their 25 and older population are small western states. By contrast, four of the five states that will see nominal or decreasing changes for this age group are northeastern states. New York is the only state in the nation that will see its 25 and older population decrease in absolute terms.

Much of the pattern that is true for the 25+ category in Table 3.1 is also true for the 18 and older population (18+ category)—western states that have smaller populations will experience the largest percentage increases. Again, all five states with the largest percentage growth for the 18+ category are western states. Three of the five states with the smallest 18 and older population changes are northeastern states, and the remaining are midwestern states. Every state in the nation will experience positive growth in its 18 and older population, with New York's growth at the lowest level in the nation at an anemic .3 percent.

THE FUTURE STATE OF POSTSECONDARY PARTICIPATION   37

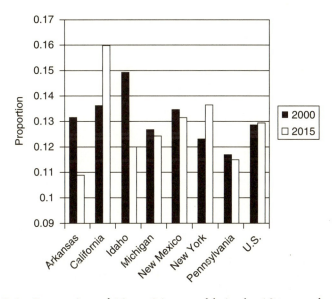

Figure 3.1   Proportion of 18- to 24-year-olds in the 18+ population.
(*Source: Author's calculations. U.S. Census 2015 projections obtained in 2002
(www.census.gov). Age group populations for 2000 from Table PCT 24, decennial census.*)

In general, states with large populations do not show as large percentage increases in population growth as smaller states, but there are exceptions. California and New Jersey, for example, are sizable states that will see dramatic growth in their 18 and older populations. Even though some states may not see dramatic population growth, shifts within that population may occur. It is possible that one age group becomes a bigger proportion of the total 18 and older population than the other age group due to different rates of growth for the two age groups that comprise the population.

Figure 3.1 shows the changes in age structure for a select group of states from Table 3.1. The figure displays the proportion of 18- to 24-year-olds in the 18 and older population for 2000 compared to the projected proportions for 2015. The seven states in the figure represent different regions of the country and demonstrate different patterns in the shifts in the 18- to 24-year-old population. It is not necessary to show the 25 and older proportional shifts, because an increase in the proportion of 18- to 24-year-olds implies a decrease in the proportion of those

25 and older. A decrease in the proportion of 18- to 24-year-olds implies an increase in the proportion of those 25 and older. The 2015 age group proportions for both age groups are shown in Appendix D for all 50 states and the nation.

The projected 30.5 million 18- to 24-year-olds in the nation will represent 13 percent of the 18 and older population in 2015, compared with 12.9 percent in 2000. Although the national proportion of adults in the two age groups will not shift significantly, there will be noticeable shifts in many of the states. The age structures in Arkansas, California, Idaho and New York will shift, as shown in Figure 3.1. In Arkansas and Idaho, 18- to 24-year-olds will become a smaller proportion of the population in 2015, but in California and New York they will become a larger proportion of the population. The proportion of 18- to 24-year-olds in Michigan, New Mexico, and Pennsylvania will remain relatively unchanged from 2000 to 2015.

The projected proportions of 18- to 24-year-olds and those 25 and older in a given state are attributed to the actual population changes in these two age groups over time. In Michigan, there will be little population growth and therefore little change between the proportional representation of the two age groups in the population. New Mexico, on the other hand, will see population growth for both age groups, but the result still will be little change between the proportional representation of the two age groups in the population. The proportional representation of the two age groups in both these states will remain relatively stable, but their projected growth patterns for the two age groups are quite different. New York, like Michigan, will see little total population growth, yet there will be a noticeable increase in the proportion of 18- to 24-year-olds in the population. The state of New York also demonstrates that a small proportional shift in the population has wide reaching implications for the future. In New York, there were 1,759,730 18- to 24-year-olds in the Year 2000, representing 12.3 percent of the 18 and older population. In 2015, this age group is projected to comprise 13.7 percent of the 18 and older population, representing a 1.4 percent increase over the Year 2000. This projected 1.4 percent proportional increase represents 198,751 people in this age range, or an 11.3 percent absolute increase over the Year 2000. An incremental shift in the proportion of 18- to 24-year-olds in New York translates into large increases in the actual population size for that group. In California, the proportional shifts will be even more dramatic than in New York. Shifts in the age structure of the states have important implications for future economic development and should be tied to educational policy (Bloom, Canning, & Sevilla, 2002) if states are to effectively plan for the future.

Projecting Baseline Enrollments for 2015

The 2015 population projections by age group can be used to calculate a Baseline scenario for future postsecondary enrollment. The 2015 baseline enrollment demand for each age group, by state, is given by the following formulas:

2015 Baseline enrollment (18–24) = 2000 Participation rate (18–24) * (number of projected 18- to 24-year-olds in 2015)

2015 Baseline enrollment (25+) = 2000 Participation rate (25+) * (number of projected persons 25+ in 2015)

The formulas to calculate 2015 baseline enrollment demand build on previous information: (a) the participation rates, which were calculated in Chapter 2 for all states and the nation, and (b) the age group population projections from Table 3.1 and Appendix C. The assumption in the Baseline scenario is that each state's participation rates are constant and will neither decrease nor increase—that is, participation rates are held at the status quo level. The Baseline scenario provides a reasonable starting point to compare current and future enrollments. Since the participation rates are constant, the only variable in projecting baseline enrollment demand is the changing age group populations.

Table 3.2 displays each component of the 2015 baseline enrollment, by age group, along with the resulting baseline enrollment demand calculation for the nation and seven sample states. The seven states in Figure 3.1 are used in Table 3.2 and throughout the rest of the chapter for illustration purposes. Future enrollment demand projections for the 50 states and the nation appear in Appendix D.

The baseline enrollments in Table 3.2 are most useful when viewed against current enrollment. Alone, baseline enrollments project the number of students the state should expect in 2015, but there is no basis for comparison. By comparing 2015 baseline enrollments against current enrollment levels, it is possible for states to gauge the expected increase or decrease in enrollment by age group. The comparison between current and future enrollments is most useful in two formats: actual numeric changes in demand and percentage changes. Numeric and percentage changes are more informative together than either alone. It is possible for a state to have a very large percentage increase in enrollment only because the original number of students was very small. Conversely, a very large state might show a very small percentage increase in enrollment, but the projected increase in the number of students is very large. Numeric changes without percentage changes cannot give states a comprehensive feel for the magnitude of enrollment shifts taking place in their higher

Table 3.2 Baseline Scenario, 2015

State	2000 Participation Rates		Projected Population for 2015		2015 Baseline Enrollment	
	18–24	25+	18–24	25+	18–24	25+
Arkansas	28.6%	3.0%	249,447	2,045,958	71,381	62,071
California	35.4%	6.4%	4,718,293	24,848,269	1,670,784	1,583,312
Idaho	30.7%	4.4%	145,439	1,066,044	44,643	46,604
Michigan	36.7%	4.6%	936,107	6,590,137	343,321	301,119
New Mexico	29.1%	6.0%	220,384	1,451,741	64,032	87,287
New York	39.5%	4.8%	1,958,481	12,379,977	774,517	590,147
Pennsylvania	39.0%	3.3%	1,116,862	8,593,689	435,939	284,084
United States	34.0%	4.5%	30,515,711	205,095,143	10,365,435	9,226,735

(*Source*: Author's calculations. U.S. Census 2015 projections obtained in 2002 (www.census.gov). Age group populations for 2000 from Table PCT 24, decennial census.)

education systems. The formulas below show how to calculate numeric and percentage changes in enrollment, using 2015 baseline enrollment demand compared to 2000 enrollment.

Numeric Changes in Enrollment:

Enrollment change (18–24) = 2015 Projected demand (18–24)
 − Current number of 18- to 24-year-olds participating in 2000

Enrollment change (25+) = 2015 Projected demand (25+)
 − Current number of people 25 and older participating in 2000

Percentage Changes in Enrollment:

Change in demand (18–24) = $\frac{\text{2015 Demand (18–24)} - \text{Current participation (18–24)}}{\text{Current participation (18–24)}}$

Change in demand (25+) = $\frac{\text{2015 Demand (25+)} - \text{Current participation (25+)}}{\text{Current participation (25+)}}$

The numeric and percentage changes in enrollment demand are shown for the seven sample states and the nation in Table 3.3. Since the baseline enrollment projections keep participation rates constant and rely on changes in the age group populations, the percentage enrollment changes mirror the percentage changes in the 2015 age group populations. The 11.3 percent enrollment increase of 18- to 24-year-olds in New York, for example, mirrors the 11.3 percent increase in 18- to 24-year-olds in the 18 and older population in the state from 2000 to 2015. The numeric and percentage changes in enrollment for all states and the nation are shown in Appendix E.

The states in Table 3.3 represent a variety of enrollment trends. California and New York's enrollment increases for the 18- to 24-year-old age group will surge if the states are able to provide the services necessary to accommodate these additional students. The additional demand from the 25 and older age group in Arkansas, Idaho, New Mexico, and Pennsylvania will be greater than the additional demand from the 18- to 24-year-old age group. In Idaho and New Mexico, students 25 and older will comprise the majority of postsecondary enrollments in 2015. In all the other states in the table, the 18- to 24-year-old student population will remain the majority.

Table 3.3 Enrollment Changes: 2000 to 2015

State	Enrollment Changes 18–24	Enrollment Changes 25+	Percentage Changes 18–24	Percentage Changes 25+
Arkansas	−3,633	9,549	−4.8%	18.2%
California	484,068	226,163	40.8%	16.7%
Idaho	2,186	12,177	5.1%	35.4%
Michigan	2,274	7,959	0.7%	2.7%
New Mexico	12,699	19,056	24.7%	27.9%
New York	78,600	−7,749	11.3%	−1.3%
Pennsylvania	8,228	10,823	1.9%	4.0%
United States	1,196,130	1,046,773	13.0%	12.8%

(*Source:* Author's calculations. U.S. Census 2015 projections obtained in 2002 (www.census.gov). Age group populations for 2000 from Table PCT 24, decennial census.)

Comparison Ratio Changes

The comparison ratios from Chapter 2 combine state participation rates and age group proportions for 2000. The formulas to calculate the 2015 comparison ratios for the Baseline scenario are similar to the formulas to calculate the 2000 comparison ratios.

Baseline Comparison Ratios

2015 Comparison ratio (18–24) = Status quo participation rate (18–24)/2015 Proportion of 18- to 24-year-olds in the 18 and older population

2015 Comparison ratio (25+) = Status quo participation rate (25+)/ 2015 Proportion of 25+ in the 18 and older population

A state's comparison ratio can change from one time period to the next if the participation rate changes, if age group demographic shifts occur, or if both participation rates and demographic shifts occur simultaneously. Baseline enrollment projections for 2015 assume a constant participation rate but changing age group demographics. The 2015 comparison ratios that correspond to the Baseline scenario therefore reflect a shift in age group demographics, not a change in the participation rate.

THE FUTURE STATE OF POSTSECONDARY PARTICIPATION 43

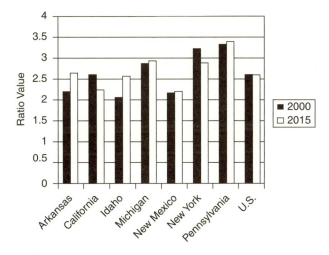

Figure 3.2 Comparison ratios for 18- to 24-year-olds. (*Source: Author's calculations. Comparison ratios constructed from Census Table P24 for participation rates and Census projections for 2015 age group demographics from www.census.gov.*)

The comparison ratio for any year reveals something about how a state's participation rates might vary from expected participation rates, given the national comparison ratio for that year. One application of the comparison ratio is to compare state results for the same year. As with the 2000 national comparison ratio, the 2015 national comparison ratio can be assessed against the 2015 comparison ratios for the individual states.

A state's comparison ratio may change from one time period to the next due to changes in age group demographics. One age group may grow faster than the other age group, which would cause a change in the age group proportions of the 18 and older population. If large shifts occur, changes in the comparison ratios will be large. It is possible that the 2015 projections result in new population figures but similar age group proportions as 2000. In these cases, the comparison ratios for the two time periods will change very little despite the population changes. States with minor population changes will not see great fluctuation in their comparison ratios either.

Figure 3.2 shows the 18- to 24-year-old comparison ratios for 2000 and 2015 for the seven sample states in Table 3.3, assuming that participation rates for 2015 are the same as for 2000. The 2000 comparison ratios are given to illustrate how a state's position relative to the national average and other states may change over time. The 25+ age group comparison ratios are not necessary to display in the graphic. A change in the 18- to 24-year-old comparison ratio automatically produces a change in the 25+ comparison ratio, but in the opposite direction. The 2015 comparison ratios for all states are shown in Appendix F.

The comparison ratio for the nation shows little change between 2000 and 2015. Nationally, the populations for 18- to 24-year-olds and those 25 and older are both projected to increase, but the increases are such that they preserve the proportional representation of the two age groups. Since the Baseline scenario also applies 2000 participation rates to 2015, the result is an unchanging national comparison ratio.

The projected demographic shifts in the states will affect state comparison ratios. For instance, Arkansas's 2000 comparison ratio for 18- to 24-year-olds was less than the national comparison ratio. This means that the participation rate for 18- to 24-year-olds in Arkansas was lower than expected. Arkansas's 18- to 24-year-old population will become a smaller proportion of the 18 and older population in 2015, thus increasing the comparison ratio value in 2015. As shown in Figure 3.2, Arkansas's 2015 comparison ratio for 18- to 24-year-olds is slightly larger than the national average. This means that if all states achieve baseline performance, Arkansas, in 2015, will be producing a higher than expected 18- to 24-year-old participation rate, given the proportion of 18- to 24-year-olds in its population. In effect, the state would be maintaining its participation rate for this age group even as it becomes a smaller proportion of the state's 18 and older population. In sum, Arkansas's participation rate for 18- to 24-year-olds in 2015 will gain ground relative to the national average if baseline performance is maintained across the states.

States may differ in their responses if they see that the value of their 2015 comparison ratio is projected to change over time. These responses would likely be based on the different values and goals of the states. One option for Arkansas is to focus on participation for the 25 and older age group since the projected growth in this age group will outpace growth for the 18- to 24-year-old age group. The state's 25+ comparison ratio for 2015 will lose ground relative to the national average (Appendix F) if the state only maintains its current participation rate while the proportion of this population is growing.

The responses in California and New York may be different than in Arkansas. In California and New York, the 18- to 24-year-old age groups will grow in proportion to the 25 and older age group. If participation rates are maintained but not improved, the 18- to 24-year-old comparison ratios in 2015 for California and New York will decrease relative to the national average, as shown in Figure 3.2. One state may view this situation as acceptable since its previous participation rate is applied to a larger population. This means more 18- to 24-year-olds would enroll in 2015 compared to 2000. Another state may view this as unacceptable and wish to improve its participation rate as the 18- to 24-year-old population grows. An improved participation rate would increase the comparison ratio for California and New York.

In Figure 3.2, the 18- to 24-year-old comparison ratios for Arkansas, Idaho, Michigan, New Mexico, and Pennsylvania have increased for 2015 relative to the national average. The proportion of 18- to 24-year-olds in these states is projected to decrease. In some of these states, the number of 18- to 24-year-olds has increased but the number of people 25 and older has increased even more. The 25+ comparison ratio for Arkansas, Idaho, Michigan, New Mexico, and Pennsylvania will decrease in 2015 if participation rates remain constant while the proportion of the 25+ age group increases. The 25+ participation rates in 2015 for these states will lose ground relative to the national average. The 25+ comparison ratios for California and New York are opposite the other five states in the figure for 2015. The status quo 25+ participation rates for these two states will look more favorable in 2015 than in 2000 since the 25 and older population will become a smaller proportion of the 18 and older population.

Conclusion

The availability of age group demographics for 2000 and 2015 makes age structure the ideal tool for helping state and higher education leaders plan for the future. The Baseline scenario for 2015 provides the necessary starting point to compare current and future enrollment. Most states across the nation will experience changing enrollment patterns in 2015. As the projected proportion of 18- to 24-year-olds and those 25 and older shifts, states will face new challenges to higher education accessibility. States will be forced to confront funding issues and revisit their previous assumptions related to postsecondary participation. A fully informed discussion should incorporate more than just one scenario, however. Chapter 4 challenges these issues even further by considering enrollment scenarios that assume states improve their participation rates rather than just maintain the status quo.

CHAPTER 4

Leave No Student Behind
Exceeding the Status Quo

Most states strive to improve postsecondary participation. A number of factors indicate that the demand for postsecondary education will increase in the future, so the question will be whether states are able to meet the demand and improve participation rates. Future demand will be fueled by a number of factors, chief among them demographic growth, educational improvements, and policy imperatives. The 2001 No Child Left Behind (NCLB) Act is an example of a policy imperative that is pressing for broad educational improvements that, if met, will significantly contribute to the demand for postsecondary education. NCLB Act is a new law and revision of the Elementary and Secondary Education Act and represents systematic reforms in elementary and secondary education in the United States. The four major areas of change include allowing for parental controls, implementing best practices based on research, increasing accountability, and expanding local control and flexibility (Department of Education, 2003). Even states with minimal demographic growth can expect increases in demand for postsecondary education if K–12 academic preparation improves. As adults respond to delivery improvements that accommodate their needs, demand also will increase.

Demographic changes, educational improvements, and policy imperatives all create a need for states to consider possible increases in postsecondary participation rates in the future and the associated impact of such improvements on higher education policy. For the purposes of this chapter, the benchmark participation rate is the highest state participation rate in the nation. Rhode Island has the highest participation rate for 18- to 24-year-olds, at 47.7 percent; California has the highest participation rate for those 25 and older (25+), at 6.4 percent. What if every state achieved benchmark participation rates for the two age groups in the future? How many students would arrive at the doors of higher education in 2015? What would states need to do to prepare for benchmark enrollment levels?

The benchmark participation rates achieved by Rhode Island and California establish a standard of performance. Other states should consider what their enrollments would look like if they provided this level of access. Every state could point to a number of barriers to such achievement, but those states that emphasize access for all do not first become paralyzed by the obstacles before they outline the possibilities.

It may be that after further assessment some states consider benchmark participation rates unattainable. However, the exercise of projecting scenarios for benchmark enrollments establishes an upper boundary, or a maximum future enrollment level, from which states can plan. The baseline established the lower boundary, or the minimum future enrollment level for the states assuming participation rates do not decline, so it is appropriate to define the maximum future enrollment level as well. With both minimum and maximum enrollment scenarios, the states have appropriate parameters from which to work.

States may also set intermediate goals that move them in the direction of the benchmark. A scenario that captures improvement beyond the baseline but below the benchmark may be of value to the states. Morrison and Wilson (1997) advocate the practice of developing various scenarios during the planning process. The authors believe that if organizations develop multiple scenarios, they are better able to remain flexible and prepare for uncertainty. The different scenarios should have descriptive titles that capture the essence of the assumptions embedded in them. Finally, Morrison and Wilson believe that any scenario must stretch the conventional wisdom yet remain plausible.

Based on the insight provided by Morrison and Wilson, this chapter offers a third future scenario to compare against the Benchmark and Baseline scenarios. The third scenario assumes each state incrementally improves on its expected participation rates by 2015, even the top performing states. For most states, the participation improvement represented by the third scenario is larger than the Baseline scenario but less than the Benchmark scenario, thus providing an intermediate scenario for comparison. This scenario, called the Baseline Plus scenario, will be discussed after the Benchmark scenario for 2015. The crux of the chapter compares the Baseline, Baseline Plus and Benchmark scenarios.

The comparison ratio introduced in Chapter 2 and pursued in Chapter 3 is not presented for the Baseline Plus and Benchmark scenarios in this chapter. The interpretation of the comparison ratios for these two scenarios is complex since the results are the product of changes in age group populations and participation rates. The enrollment comparisons across the three scenarios sufficiently demonstrate the effect of multiple changes on projected demand in a more straightforward manner. The comparison ratios for the Baseline Plus and Benchmark scenarios are included in Appendix F for states that have an interest in pursuing additional analysis.

Benchmark Achievement

The central assumption in Chapter 3 was that states maintain their current participation rates in the future. The Baseline scenario in Chapter 3 showed state enrollment levels for 2015, assuming these status quo participation rates. In order to improve baseline enrollment levels for 2015, states would have to improve their participation rates in the future. The Benchmark scenario assumes that in 2015 every state achieves a participation rate equal to the 2000 benchmark participation rate for each age group. The benchmark participation rate can be multiplied by each state's 2015 age group population to show 2015 state benchmark enrollment for each age group. The calculation for state benchmark enrollment is shown below for each age group.

2015 Benchmark enrollment (18–24) = 47.7% * (number of projected persons 18 to 24 in 2015)

2015 Benchmark enrollment (25+) = 6.4% * (number of projected persons 25+ in 2015)

Rhode Island's benchmark participation rate of 47.7 percent for 18- to 24-year-olds is applied to every state's 18- to 24-year-old projected population to calculate benchmark enrollment by state. California's 25+ benchmark participation rate of 6.4 percent is applied to every state's 25 and older projected population to calculate benchmark enrollment by state.

The population projections for each state are the same as those used in Chapter 3 to calculate baseline enrollment. In the Baseline scenario, the resulting enrollment changes were attributed to changes in the age group populations only. The participation rate was held constant in the Baseline scenario so did not contribute to the changing enrollments. In the Benchmark scenario for each state, both the age group populations and the participation rates contribute to the benchmark enrollment projections. The age group populations are the same as those used in the

Baseline scenario, but they are still different from the 2000 age group populations. The participation rates also change for the Benchmark scenarios, as each state's assumed participation rate is not status quo but equivalent to the best performing state in the nation.

Once the benchmark enrollment projections are calculated, states can compare their Benchmark and Baseline scenarios. This comparison offers states a perspective on how status quo assumptions differ from the top performance assumptions embedded in the Benchmark scenario. The difference between a state's projected benchmark enrollment and its projected baseline enrollment is referred to in this chapter as the participation gap.

Participation gap (18–24) = 2015 Enrollment at benchmark participation rate (18–24)
 −2015 Baseline enrollment (18–24)

Participation gap (25+) = 2015 Enrollment at benchmark participation rate (25+)
 −2015 Baseline enrollment (25+)

Every state will have a participation gap for each age group, except the top performing state for each age group. States with the largest participation gaps are those with the largest differences between their status quo participation rates and the benchmark participation rates. The participation gap is best analyzed by age group. Table 4.1 compares baseline and benchmark enrollments for the 18- to 24-year-old age group for 10 states. Also shown in the table are the associated participation gaps and the percentage changes in enrollment from benchmark to baseline. Appendix G contains data for the remaining states and the nation for this age group.

The first five states in Table 4.1 are those with the largest participation gaps relative to their baseline enrollments. The last five states are those with the smallest participation gaps relative to their baseline enrollments. For the first five states, the magnitude of the participation gap is formidable. These states would likely have to consider new fiscal strategies for funding higher education and increase capacity to accommodate their respective benchmark enrollments. For example, in Nevada the participation gap is 47,571 students, which is larger than the 2015 baseline enrollment. The baseline enrollment of 41,805 students is what Nevada can expect if it continues to provide enough resources to maintain its existing level of higher education services and does nothing else to decrease or increase its participation rate for 18- to 24-year-olds. The additional 47,571 students represented by the participation gap means

Table 4.1 Comparison of 2015 Baseline and Benchmark Scenarios for 18- to 24-Year-Olds

State	Baseline Enrollment	Benchmark Enrollment	Participation Gap	% Change (Gap/Baseline)
Alaska	16,863	41,920	25,057	148.6%
Nevada	41,805	89,376	47,571	113.8%
Georgia	262,039	447,996	185,957	71.0%
Arkansas	71,381	119,085	47,703	66.8%
Texas	759,156	1,260,299	501,142	66.0%
Iowa	107,117	127,673	20,555	19.2%
Vermont	25,467	28,238	2,771	10.9%
North Dakota	31,085	33,672	2,587	8.3%
Massachusetts	300,821	325,299	24,478	8.1%
Rhode Island	51,633	51,633	0	0.0%

(*Source:* Author's calculations. U.S. Census 2015 projections obtained in 2002 (www.census.gov). Age group populations for 2000 from Table PCT 24, decennial census.)

that the state would have to provide additional resources to increase higher education services if it hopes to close its participation gap. Texas, though much larger than Nevada, would have to accommodate an additional half-million students in 2015 to fill its participation gap.

The bottom five states in the table had high 2000 participation rates for 18- to 24-year-olds, so the level of improvement needed to reach the benchmark participation rate is small relative to the top five states in the table. The result is that the participation gap for the bottom five states is also comparatively small. None of the bottom five states in the table would have to accommodate more than a 19.2 percent enrollment increase to reach benchmark enrollment levels by 2015. Three of the last five states in the table are located in the northeastern United States. In general, northeastern states have higher 2000 participation rates for the 18- to 24-year-old age group than western states.

Table 4.2 compares baseline and benchmark enrollments for the 25+ age group for 10 states. Also shown in the table are the associated participation gaps and the percentage changes in enrollment from benchmark to baseline. Appendix H contains data for the remaining states and the nation for this age group.

Table 4.2 Comparison of 2015 Baseline and Benchmark Scenarios for 25 and Older

State	Baseline Enrollment	Benchmark Enrollment	Participation Gap	% Change (Gap/Baseline)
West Virginia	37,602	84,976	47,374	126.0%
Arkansas	62,071	130,367	68,296	110.0%
Mississippi	62,110	127,682	65,571	105.6%
Tennessee	143,337	279,027	135,690	94.7%
Kentucky	97,130	187,645	90,516	93.2%
Arizona	210,395	242,872	32,477	15.4%
Alaska	25,762	29,399	3,637	14.1%
Utah	89,996	99,315	9,318	10.4%
New Mexico	87,287	92,504	5,216	6.0%
California	1,583,312	1,583,312	—	0.0%

(*Source*: Author's calculations. U.S. Census 2015 projections obtained in 2002 (www.census.gov). Age group populations for 2000 from Table PCT 24, decennial census.)

The first five states in Table 4.2 are those with the largest participation gaps relative to their baseline enrollments. The last five states are those with the smallest participation gaps relative to their baseline enrollments. Much like the states with the largest participation gaps for the 18- to 24-year-old age group, the states with the largest participation gaps for the 25+ age group would likely have to consider new fiscal strategies for funding higher education and increase capacity to accommodate their respective benchmark enrollments. The participation gaps for West Virginia, Arkansas, and Mississippi are larger than their 2015 baseline enrollments. These states would have to provide additional resources to increase higher education services if they hope to close their participation gaps.

The bottom five states in the table had high 2000 participation rates for the 25 and older population, so the level of improvement needed to reach the benchmark participation rate is not significant. The result is that the participation gaps for these states are rather modest. None of the bottom five states in the table would have to accommodate more than a 15.4 percent increase in students to reach benchmark enrollment levels by 2015.

Table 4.3 Comparison of 2015 Baseline and Benchmark Scenarios for 18 and Older

State	Baseline Enrollment	Benchmark Enrollment	Participation Gap	% Change (Gap/Baseline)
Arkansas	133,453	249,452	115,999	86.9%
West Virginia	88,498	158,243	69,745	78.8%
Kentucky	210,454	370,999	160,545	76.3%
Tennessee	322,795	564,882	242,086	75.0%
Mississippi	154,212	268,133	113,920	73.9%
Maryland	419,367	520,447	101,079	24.1%
Utah	205,988	250,669	44,681	21.7%
California	3,254,096	3,835,801	581,705	17.9%
Massachusetts	524,441	607,475	83,034	15.8%
Rhode Island	85,695	97,152	11,457	13.4%

(*Source:* Author's calculations. U.S. Census 2015 projections obtained in 2002 (www.census.gov). Age group populations for 2000 from Table PCT 24, decennial census.)

The regional patterns in Table 4.2 are striking. The last five states in the table are located in the western United States. The first five states are southern states. There are undoubtedly a number of factors that contribute to this regional outcome, one of which is certainly the presence in many western states of a developed two-year sector.

Table 4.3 combines the two previous tables to compare baseline and benchmark enrollments for all adults 18 and older for 10 states. Also shown in the table are the associated participation gaps and the percentage changes in enrollment from benchmark to baseline. Appendix I contains data for the remaining states and the nation for this population.

The first five states listed in Table 4.3 are those with the largest participation gaps relative to their baseline enrollments. The last five states are those with the smallest participation gaps relative to their baseline enrollments. The first five states in the table are all southern states. These states all had large participation gaps for the 25+ age group and significant participation gaps for the 18- to 24-year-old age group. The five states at the bottom of the table have the smallest participation gaps for the 18 and older population in their states. The states with the smallest total participation gaps either had benchmark or near benchmark participation rates for one of the age groups or strong participation rates for both age groups. Massachusetts and Maryland are examples of states that did not achieve the benchmark participation rate for either age group, but their participation rates for both age groups were well above the national averages. Some states such as California have a small participation gap in percentage terms, but the magnitude of the absolute participation gap (581,705) cannot be minimized and will certainly present challenges to higher education policy if the state strives to meet such demand.

Moving Toward Improvement

For many states, it may be difficult to achieve benchmark participation rates by 2015. These states should still use the benchmark participation rates to establish an upper enrollment limit for planning purposes. States may also set enrollment goals that go beyond the projected Baseline scenario but remain below the Benchmark scenario. The degree of improvement that a state might wish to achieve is a function of many factors, some of which include resources, state policy goals, or simply the preferences of the most influential actors in the state.

Setting an improvement goal is important for two reasons. First, improvement goals recognize that even top performing states should strive for better performance. In this sense, improvement is relative to a state's past performance and is not tied to the achievement levels of other states. Second, an improvement goal that accompanies the Baseline and Benchmark scenarios provides a third projection for each state. The scenario that contains improvement over the baseline is called the "Baseline Plus" scenario in this chapter. The Baseline Plus scenario assumes that each state improves its participation rates 20 percent by the year 2015. The 20 percent increase represents an annual improvement of approximately 1.33 percent (20%/15 years). This annual improvement represents Weick's (1984) notion that it is a series of small wins that eventually leads to a significant improvement over time.

Improvement goals are often conservative and incremental but may range by state. The Baseline Plus scenario is thus a moderate goal and one example of enrollments that lie between baseline and benchmark enrollments. Some states may want to target an increase that is different from the 20 percent represented by the Baseline Plus scenario. Such a scenario would replace or accompany the Baseline Plus scenario if that is what makes sense for a particular state. The goal of continual improvement above status quo assumptions is what is important to capture, whatever additional scenario a state may choose.

The Baseline Plus scenario challenges states to stretch beyond the status quo, or the Baseline scenario. For some states, that will mean moving toward benchmark performance but not surpassing it. For those states with already high participation rates, the Baseline Plus scenario will represent a challenge to improve already strong performance. Since the Baseline Plus scenario for every state assumes a 20 percent improvement over the Baseline scenario, there is no way to rank which states require the largest or smallest levels of improvement between the Baseline and Baseline Plus scenarios. For continuity, the states in Tables 4.1, 4.2, and 4.3 will illustrate baseline plus enrollments for the corresponding age groups. The Baseline Plus scenario will also be compared to the Baseline and Benchmark scenarios.

Baseline Plus

The Baseline Plus scenario for each state assumes that each state improves its participation rate 20 percent above its 2000 participation rate, even those states that are at benchmark performance. If the participation rate increases by 20 percent by 2015, then the 2015 baseline plus enrollment will be 20 percent greater than the baseline enrollment for every state. The Baseline Plus scenario for each state, by age group, is calculated by the following formulas.

2015 Baseline plus enrollment (18–24) = (2000 State participation rate (18–24) * 1.20) * (number of projected persons 18 to 24 in 2015)

2015 Baseline plus enrollment (25+) = (2000 State participation rate (25+) * 1.20) * (number of projected persons 25+ in 2015)

Table 4.4 compares baseline, baseline plus, and benchmark enrollments for the 18- to 24-year-old age group for 10 states. The 10 states in Table 4.4 are from Table 4.1. The baseline plus enrollments and participation rates for all states are 20 percent greater than the baseline enrollments and participation rates. Appendix G contains data for the remaining states and the nation for this age group.

Baseline plus enrollments for 45 of the 50 states are less than the benchmark enrollments. For many of these states, particularly the first five states listed in Table 4.4, achieving benchmark enrollments may seem impossible. The Baseline Plus scenario provides a target enrollment

Table 4.4 Comparison of 2015 Baseline, Baseline Plus, and Benchmark Scenarios for 18- to 24-Year-Olds

State	Baseline Enrollment	Baseline Plus Enrollment	Benchmark Enrollment	Baseline to Baseline Plus	Baseline to Benchmark
Alaska	16,863	20,235	41,920	3,372	25,057
Nevada	41,805	50,166	89,376	8,361	47,571
Georgia	262,039	314,446	447,996	52,407	185,957
Arkansas	71,381	85,657	119,085	14,276	47,703
Texas	759,156	910,988	1,260,299	151,832	501,142
Iowa	107,117	128,541	127,673	21,424	20,555
Vermont	25,467	30,561	28,238	5,094	2,771
North Dakota	31,085	37,302	33,672	6,217	2,587
Massachusetts	300,821	360,985	325,299	60,164	24,478
Rhode Island	51,633	61,960	51,633	10,327	0

(*Source:* Author's calculations. U.S. Census 2015 projections obtained in 2002 (www.census.gov). Age group populations for 2000 from Table PCT 24, decennial census.)

below the benchmark but above the baseline. In the state of Georgia, the Baseline Plus scenario calls for an additional 52,407 students above the Baseline scenario. The baseline enrollment of 262,039 students is what Georgia can expect if it continues to provide enough resources to maintain its existing level of higher education services and does nothing else to decrease or increase its participation rate for 18- to 24-year-olds. The additional 52,407 students represented by the Baseline Plus scenario means that the state would have to provide additional resources to increase higher education services if it hopes to improve beyond the status quo. The Baseline Plus scenario represents an achievable goal for those states that may view the Benchmark scenario as too aggressive.

The last five states in Table 4.4 had high 2000 participation rates for 18- to 24-year-olds, so the added enrollments to reach benchmark levels were very incremental. These are the only five states for which the 20 percent baseline plus improvement in enrollment is actually more than the benchmark enrollment. In these cases, the Baseline Plus scenario serves as an incentive for these states to continually improve their participation rates for the 18- to 24-year-old population. The modest 1.33 percent annual increase still holds for these states, but it is more

Table 4.5 Comparison of 2015 Baseline, Baseline Plus, and Benchmark Scenarios for 25 and Older

State	Baseline Enrollment	Baseline Plus Enrollment	Benchmark Enrollment	Baseline to Baseline Plus	Baseline to Benchmark
West Virginia	37,602	45,122	84,976	7,520	47,374
Arkansas	62,071	74,486	130,367	12,415	68,296
Mississippi	62,110	74,532	127,682	12,422	65,571
Tennessee	143,337	172,005	279,027	28,668	135,690
Kentucky	97,130	116,556	187,645	19,426	90,516
Arizona	210,395	252,474	242,872	42,079	32,477
Alaska	25,762	30,914	29,399	5,152	3,637
Utah	89,996	107,996	99,315	18,000	9,318
New Mexico	87,287	104,745	92,504	17,458	5,216
California	1,583,312	1,899,974	1,583,312	316,662	0

(*Source:* Author's calculations. U.S. Census 2015 projections obtained in 2002 (www.census.gov). Age group populations for 2000 from Table PCT 24, decennial census.)

demanding than what would be required for them to reach benchmark enrollment levels.

Table 4.5 compares baseline, baseline plus, and benchmark enrollments for the 25+ age group for 10 states. The 10 states in Table 4.5 are from Table 4.2. The baseline plus enrollments and participation rates for all states are 20 percent greater than the baseline enrollments and participation rates. Appendix H contains data for the remaining states and the nation for this age group.

As with the 18- to 24-year-old age group, the states vary with regard to how much their baseline plus and benchmark enrollments differ. The first five states in Table 4.5 historically have had low participation rates for the 25 and older population, relative to the rest of the nation. The first three states in the table would have to double their enrollments for this age group to reach benchmark enrollment levels. The Baseline Plus scenario for the 25+ age group provides a target enrollment below the benchmark but above the baseline. West Virginia had the lowest 25+ participation rate of all states in 2000. The state would have to realize a 126 percent increase above its baseline enrollment to reach benchmark enrollment. The state's 20 percent increase

Table 4.6 Comparison of 2015 Baseline, Baseline Plus, and Benchmark Scenarios for 18 and Older

State	Baseline Enrollment	Baseline Plus Enrollment	Benchmark Enrollment	Baseline to Baseline Plus	Baseline to Benchmark
Arkansas	133,453	160,143	249,452	26,690	115,999
West Virginia	88,498	106,198	158,243	17,700	69,745
Kentucky	210,454	252,545	370,999	42,091	160,545
Tennessee	322,795	387,355	564,882	64,560	242,086
Mississippi	154,212	185,055	268,133	30,843	113,920
Maryland	419,367	503,241	520,447	83,874	101,079
Utah	205,988	247,185	250,669	41,197	44,681
California	3,254,096	3,904,915	3,835,801	650,819	581,705
Massachusetts	524,441	629,329	607,475	104,888	83,034
Rhode Island	85,695	102,834	97,152	17,139	11,457

(*Source:* Author's calculations. U.S. Census 2015 projections obtained in 2002 (www.census.gov). Age group populations for 2000 from Table PCT 24, decennial census.)

represented by the Baseline Plus scenario is not as aggressive as the benchmark enrollment target, but it includes 7,520 students above the baseline enrollment of 37,602 students. If the Baseline Plus scenario seems too modest for West Virginia, an appropriate target may lie somewhere between the Baseline Plus and Benchmark scenarios.

The last five states in Table 4.5 had very high 2000 participation rates for the 25+ age group, so the added enrollments to reach benchmark levels represent minimal improvement. The 20 percent baseline plus enrollments are more than the benchmark enrollments for all five of these states. The modest 1.33 percent annual increase required to reach the final baseline plus enrollments is more demanding than what would be required to reach benchmark enrollments. The Baseline Plus scenario for these states represents a challenge to improve already strong performance.

Table 4.6 compares baseline, baseline plus, and benchmark enrollments for the 18 and older population for 10 states. The information for each state in Table 4.6 is the total for the 18- to 24-year-old enrollments and 25+ enrollments. Table 4.6 therefore represents total postsecondary enrollment for the states for each scenario. The 10 states in Table 4.6 are from Table 4.3. The baseline plus enrollments and participation rates for all states are 20 percent greater than the baseline enrollments and participation rates. Appendix I contains data for the remaining states and the nation for this age group.

The 18 and older enrollment scenarios are affected by the shifting populations for both age groups. Some states will have difficulty meeting the enrollment demands of the growing traditional student population but not the adult student population. The participation rate for 18- to 24-year-olds in these states will lose ground relative to the national average. Other states will have difficulty meeting the enrollment demands of the growing adult student population but not the traditional student population. The participation rate for the 25+ age group in these states will lose ground relative to the national average. States that produce strong results for one age group but weak results for the other are not represented in Table 4.6. For these states, a strong performance for one age group somewhat compensates for a weak performance for the other age group. Generally, such states do not produce the highest variations between baseline and benchmark enrollments. States that produce close to average participation rates for both age groups also would not show as much variation between baseline and benchmark enrollments as those states shown in Table 4.6.

The five states listed at the bottom of Table 4.6 had high 2000 participation rates for both age groups. The result for California, Massachusetts, and Rhode Island is that their total baseline plus enrollment projections are greater than their benchmark enrollment projections. Conversely, states that produce low 2000 participation rates for both age groups produce large gaps between baseline and benchmark enrollments. The five states listed at the top of Table 4.6 have below national average participation rates for both age groups and large differences between baseline plus and benchmark enrollments. The Baseline Plus scenario for these states provides a target enrollment level that is a noticeable improvement over status quo enrollments. The Baseline Plus scenario may represent a starting point for these states, as they consider the extent of improvement that they wish to target in the future.

Conclusion

Age group shifts will impact the demand for higher education in the future. States with a growing 18- to 24-year-old population will experience a growing demand for enrollment from this age group. States with a growing 25 and older population will experience a growing demand for enrollment from this age group. In some states, the population for both age groups will increase, and the intensity of demand by age group will depend on the growth rate of each age group. The shifts in state demographics must be an important consideration for policymakers, as they weigh different strategies to accommodate changing enrollments. For example, as Chapter 7 will discuss, some states may wish to emphasize growth in certain types of institutions rather than others, depending on the nature of the future demand.

One thing is certain: the level of success states achieve in meeting future postsecondary demand will be influenced by the policies they choose to employ to meet that demand. The results of these policies will manifest themselves in the states' actual 2015 participation rates. The three scenarios in this chapter offer a look into the future, assuming different rates of participation. The comparisons among the scenarios emphasize the important role that state policy must play if states are to meet the future demand for higher education. Some states will face formidable challenges as they try to meet future demand while the obstacles in other states do not seem so imposing. In any case and for every state, the various scenarios are ultimately meant to be tools for planning and policy discussion. They inform states of the magnitude of future postsecondary enrollment demand they might expect and how the two age groups contribute to that demand. Chapter 5 now turns to the fiscal implications of the various scenarios in comparison with how the states currently provide for their postsecondary needs.

CHAPTER 5

Funding Higher Education in the Future

State higher education funding is one of the primary tools policymakers use that influence access. The current and future participation statistics from the previous chapters include both the public and private sectors, but most state funding supports public institutions. Some states do specifically provide public money to subsidize private institutions or aid students who attend private institutions. This chapter utilizes current and historical state higher education funding statistics as reported by the Grapevine (2003) publication, which provides state-by-state higher education funding appropriations. The Grapevine captures student aid and operating expenses to both public and private institutions. Though state funding is largely channeled to public institutions, state higher education finance is such a prominent feature of higher education policy that it merits specific treatment and is the subject of this chapter.

In a perfect world, higher education would have access to unlimited state resources. Gold (1995) highlighted the real world of the early 1990s recession, pointing out that higher education declined while significant state spending increases were channeled to medicaid. The reality has always been that the allocation of state resources is a zero-sum game. If money is appropriated to one state agency, then there is less funding for other agencies. States set priorities, and legislators commonly view higher education as a discretionary budget item (Hovey, 1999). The result of this discretionary status is that higher education is more susceptible to funding fluctuations than other state agencies. Public institutions suffer disproportionately during economic recessions and raise tuition at precisely the time when families can least afford it; and during economic booms, public institutions benefit disproportionately and tuition stabilizes (Hauptman, 1997).

Economic cycles will continue onto 2015, and higher education funding will continue to fluctuate. Despite economic uncertainty, it is possible to use historical funding data and projected student enrollments to get a sense of future funding needs. Higher education funding and enrollment projections provide valuable information as states consider policy options to maximize access given their available resources.

This chapter explains the rationale for drawing on 2015 enrollment projections to predict future higher education funding needs. The three enrollment scenarios from the previous chapters yield different rates of enrollment growth relative to 2000 enrollment levels. These different rates of enrollment growth produce a range of funding possibilities. The funding scenarios associated with the different rates of enrollment growth demonstrate the various levels of resource commitment states would need to achieve different levels of access.

Future funding projections must also incorporate assumptions for inflation or a factor that includes inflation and associated workload costs. Three possibilities are discussed for application in this chapter: (1) Hovey's (1999) embedded assumptions in his eight-year projection of what it would take to maintain higher education spending; (2) the Consumer Price Index (CPI); and (3) the Higher Education Price Index (HEPI), which is a higher education specific measure of inflation.

Once the funding projections are calculated, an important, practical question remains: Are these funding levels possible to achieve for the states? Historical funding data provide a perspective on this important long-term question. Projected funding growth from 2000 to 2015 will be contrasted with the historical growth in funding from 1985 to 2000.[9]

The funding projections presented in this chapter are meant to establish broad parameters around the fiscal requirements that will be needed to expand higher education access in the future. And just as enrollment demand in 2015 may be affected by any number of unpredictable factors, so too might 2015 projected funding. Technology and innovation may produce the means by which education is delivered to every corner of every state at minimal cost, or they may produce the means but increase the costs. Institutions may realize economies of scale and become more efficient, driven by state accountability or their own initiative. Diverse student needs may require more state and institutional resources. Though the possibilities are endless, the funding and enrollment projections provide a starting point from which to plan. Successful states will look at the parameters that enrollment and funding projections offer as they remain flexible yet resolute on meeting the future.

Enrollment Growth

Baseline budget predictions for a particular state function commonly incorporate caseload growth and measure how much a state would have to spend to maintain the existing level of services, accounting for inflation and changes in workload (Gold, 1995, pp. 48–49). In higher education, caseload growth is equivalent to enrollment growth. Although many states no longer subscribe to an allocation strategy of funding formulas predicated on enrollments, there is an ongoing connection between enrollment and funding. Hossler, Lund, Ramin, Westfall, and Irish (1997) found that, among other variables associated with state funding, enrollment was statistically significant but not insightful. The lack of insight is because of the obvious connection between funding and enrollment: the larger the state's enrollment, the larger the appropriation. Many states that have abandoned an enrollment formula now have a "base" level of funding. This base is in theory increased every year to accommodate inflation and workload changes. The original base was usually determined by looking at historical funding, which in most cases was predicated on enrollment. New Jersey and South Dakota are examples of states that have established a base level of funding for higher education.

Future funding scenarios should account for changes in enrollment. Future funding projections that incorporate changing enrollments also preserve Gold's (1995) advice by accounting for caseload growth. The enrollment growth between 2000 enrollment and a projected enrollment is the percentage difference between the two enrollment levels. Each enrollment scenario (Baseline, Baseline Plus, and Benchmark) will produce a different "enrollment growth factor" when compared to 2000 enrollment. The enrollment growth factor for each scenario and state is total enrollment growth, which includes growth for the traditional student population and the adult student population. For purposes of analysis, enrollment growth is considered equal across all higher education sectors and levels. The enrollment growth factor for each scenario can be multiplied by 2000 state appropriations to estimate future funding needs. The 2000 appropriations used to project future funding are from the Grapevine[10] and include appropriations for operating expenses and student aid.

Funding projections in the chapter are not calculated on a per student basis. The application of one enrollment growth factor to total 2000 state appropriations assumes that future funding per student equals current funding per student. In addition, future students will receive the same level of higher education services as current students under this assumption. There are many factors that could increase or decrease efficiencies in funding per student, but absent specific information about such factors, funding per student should be held constant. A state-level analysis also avoids the complexity of detailing different student funding levels based on whether students are graduate or undergraduate students, whether they are in two- or four-year institutions, or whether they are in public or private institutions.

The enrollment and funding increases are assumed to preserve the current attendance patterns within the states as well. This means that student representation by sector and level is the same in 2015 as 2000. If a state's two-year sector enrolled 40 percent of the student population in 2000, the funding projection assumes that 40 percent of the student population will be enrolled in the two-year sector in 2015. The results of the funding and enrollment projections may compel some states to design state policies to shift students from one sector to another. New policy considerations may be motivated by the shifting demographic patterns between the two age groups or a state's perceived ability to meet future funding needs. In addition, as new policy considerations surface, the reality of differential per student costs at the two- and four-year levels must be noted. For example, states generally pay more for students who attend a four-year institution than a two-year institution. This fiscal reality may influence the policies states pursue as they consider their ability to fund higher education.

For ease of presentation, five of the seven states displayed throughout Chapter 3 are used for illustration purposes in this chapter. The mix of states still represents different regions of the country and demonstrates different patterns in the demographic shifts that will take place in 2015. Figure 5.1 shows the enrollment growth factors for the three enrollment scenarios for the five sample states. The enrollment growth factor for each scenario and state is the percentage growth of 2015 projections over actual 2000 enrollment. Appendix J shows the enrollment growth factors for the three enrollment scenarios for all 50 states.

Figure 5.1 shows how enrollment growth varies across the three scenarios for the five sample states. The baseline enrollment projections for California and Idaho are large relative to 2000 enrollment levels, due to the projected population increases. The enrollment growth factor associated with the Baseline scenario is large for these two states as a result. In California, it is the projected growth in the 18- to 24-year-old age group that will propel demand, while in Idaho most of the growth will occur in the 25+ age group. California and Idaho will have to increase funding more aggressively than the other three states shown in Figure 5.1 to maintain current service levels at the 2015 baseline enroll-

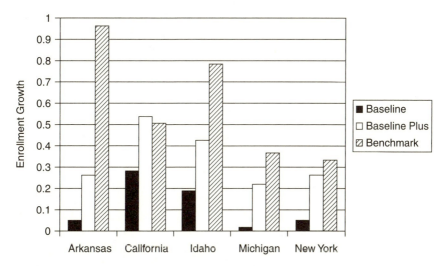

Figure 5.1 Enrollment growth factors: 2000–2015. (*Note: The calculation for the enrollment growth factors uses 2000 enrollment from decennial census and 2015 enrollment projections from the Baseline, Baseline Plus, and Benchmark scenarios.*)

ment level. The overall baseline enrollment growth in Arkansas, Michigan, and New York is modest due to slow population growth in one or both of the college-eligible age groups. In New York, the projected demand increase from the 18- to 24-year-old population will largely be offset by lower demand from the decreasing 25 and older population.

The baseline plus enrollment growth rates are larger than the baseline enrollment growth rates for every state since baseline plus enrollments are by definition 20 percent greater than baseline enrollments. The benchmark enrollment growth rates represent the highest enrollment growth rates of all three scenarios for every state in Figure 5.1 except California. California's nation-leading participation rate for the adult student population is the benchmark, so the 20 percent baseline plus improvement in enrollment is greater than the benchmark enrollment for the state.

The enrollment growth factors shown in Figure 5.1 indicate the need for additional state resources for higher education in the future. The need for additional resources is even greater for states that wish to improve access and reach baseline plus or benchmark enrollment levels. Enrollment growth is one of two factors used to project 2015 funding in this chapter; inflation is the second. There are various alternatives that capture the effects of inflation. The next section compares three alternatives that capture the effects of inflation, compares them, and suggests which is most applicable to help project future higher education funding.

The Inflation Factor

State budgeting practices commonly incorporate inflation assumptions to help higher education and other state agencies maintain their services. Inflation is the increase in the average level of prices of goods and services over time. Inflation measures are used by government and business to capture the change in prices over time. Changing prices change the buying power of the dollar. As prices rise, for example, the buying power of the dollar decreases. In higher education, inflation has consequences for students, institutions, and states. Inflation may result in higher tuition charges for students. Inflation also contributes to the increased costs that institutions incur to operate. In addition, since some research studies (The Institute for Higher Education Policy, 1999) have found that declining public revenues contribute to higher tuition prices, it might be reasonable to assume that tuition increases can be moderated by adequate state funding.

The Consumer Price Index (CPI) is the most well-known inflation measure in the United States. The CPI is a very broad measure of inflation that gauges the change in the prices of a wide variety of goods and services in the country. The goods and services included in the CPI range from food and beverages to medical care and college tuition. The U.S. Department of Labor, Bureau of Labor Statistics (www.bls.gov), tracks monthly and yearly changes in the CPI and makes this information readily available to the public.

Higher education advocates often argue against applying CPI growth rates to higher education budget projections, postulating that higher education prices rise faster than what is captured by the CPI. In response to this concern, Halstead (Research Associates of Washington, 2003) developed the Higher Education Price Index (HEPI), which measures the average level of price changes for goods and services purchased by postsecondary institutions. The HEPI factors in changes in the CPI and services specific to higher education, such as personnel costs and library acquisitions. The HEPI has a relatively long history in its own right and as such can be compared to historical changes in the CPI. One study found that over the 20-year period from 1980 to 2000, the CPI rose 118 percent, while the HEPI rose 154 percent. The study also encouraged analysts and researchers to use the historical record of the HEPI to estimate future budget requirements (Research Associates of Washington, 2003).

Inflation assumptions projected into the future are often based on historical patterns of inflation. Funding projections in this chapter are for 15 years forward, from 2000 to 2015. The historical changes in inflation, as measured by either the CPI or the HEPI, are available from 1985 to 2000. Thus, one way to account for inflation is to assume that the previous 15-year growth rate in the CPI or HEPI will be the same over the next 15 years. This growth rate can then be applied to current higher education funding to estimate the effect of inflation on future higher education funding. Figure 5.2 displays the growth in the CPI and the HEPI from 1985 to 2000. The actual index values for the CPI and HEPI are given for the 15 years in the figure. The bottom of the figure shows the 15-year growth rate for each measure of inflation.

It is no surprise that the growth in the HEPI has outpaced the growth in the CPI. The prices of goods and services captured by the HEPI generally rise faster than those captured by the CPI. Still, the 15-year growth rates

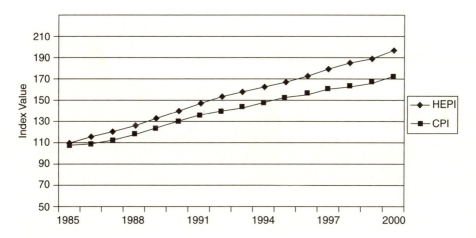

Growth from 1985–2000:
HEPI = 77.7%; CPI = 60.0%

Figure 5.2 Growth in two measures of inflation: 1985–2000. (*Source: Author's calculations. CPI figures obtained from the U.S. Department of Labor, Bureau of Labor Statistics. HEPI figures obtained from the Institution of Research and Planning at the University of Texas at Brownsville (http://ntmain.utb.edu/irp/Environ/hepi.htm), which uses 1983 as the base year with an index value of 100.*)

for the two measures are not grossly divergent. The calculated average yearly growth rate over the 15-year time period shown in Figure 5.2, from 1985 to 2000, was 4.0 percent for the HEPI and 3.2 percent for the CPI.

Both measures in Figure 5.2 capture a rise in prices over time, something that should be reflected in future higher education appropriation projections. One question arising from this analysis is whether there is another alternative to capture the rise in prices of higher education goods and services that is preferable to either the CPI or the HEPI. Hovey's (1999) eight-year projection of what it would take to maintain higher education spending factored in general inflation associated with student cost increases and presumed increases in higher education salaries. Hovey found that the net effect of these factors was that spending would have to increase a projected 6 percent per year to maintain current services. The annual 6 percent growth rate presents a competing alternative to the CPI and the HEPI.

The best inflation assumption depends on the nature of the study to which the assumption is applied. The three competing alternatives each have points of strength and weakness. The HEPI is used in this chapter because it captures two issues that Gold (1995) says are important when projecting into the future: price and workload increases. Because the original construction of the HEPI was tailored to the higher education industry, it more strongly reflects the goods and services associated with higher education. The CPI is broad and covers too many goods and services that are outside the domain of the higher education industry. Finally, the 6 percent annual increase from the Hovey (1999) report was predicated on a different set of enrollment projections for a different time period than was presented in Chapters 3, 4, and 5. In the end, the inflation factor associated with the HEPI is less than the factor Hovey derived but more than what would be applied using the CPI, probably a reasonable middle ground assumption.

Future Funding Scenarios

The Baseline, Baseline Plus, and Benchmark scenarios produce different funding estimates for 2015 for every state. The inflation assumption is applied equally to every state and all three funding scenarios. The effect of the HEPI on state appropriations from 2000 to 2015 is the historical 77.7 percent increase shown in Figure 5.2. Absent other information, historical inflation patterns are assumed to apply to the future.

The assumed 77.7 percent growth in inflation will increase the 2015 funding projection over the actual 2000 appropriation for each state.

The formula projects 2015 funding and factors in the inflation assumption. The HEPI inflation increase is applied to all 50 states equally.

2015 Funding = (2000 Appropriation) * (1.777)

The total 2015 funding projection for each state must capture both inflation and enrollment growth. The three equations below project 2015 higher education appropriations and include both inflation and enrollment growth factors. Three different equations are needed, one for each scenario. The demographic age group projections by state and the different participation rate assumptions by scenario produce different enrollment growth factors for each scenario for every state. These enrollment growth factors are included in the general formulas below. The general formulas are applicable to all 50 states.

2015 Baseline funding = (2000 Appropriation) * (Baseline enrollment growth factor) * (1.777)

2015 Baseline plus funding = (2000 Appropriation) * (Baseline plus enrollment growth factor) * (1.777)

2015 Benchmark funding = (2000 Appropriation) * (Benchmark enrollment growth factor) * (1.777)

The difference between the 2015 appropriation for each scenario and the 2000 appropriation represents the increase that states would have to provide to maintain current higher education service levels to the students represented under each scenario. Table 5.1 shows actual 2000 appropriations and 2015 funding projections for the three different scenarios for the five sample states. The funding projections in Table 5.1 are in dollar units and provide a sense of the sheer size of how much funding must grow over time. Appendix K shows the funding projections for all 50 states.

In three of the five states in Table 5.1, higher education was a billion dollar business in 2000. Arkansas higher education may well become a billion dollar business by 2015 if funding keeps pace with enrollment growth and inflation. At first glance, the required 2015 funding levels look quite imposing, especially for the Benchmark scenario. In every state, 2015 benchmark funding is more than double—and in some cases triple—the 2000 appropriations. In some states, the Baseline Plus scenario also is double the 2000 appropriation levels. Even the Baseline funding scenarios show large increases over the 2000 appropriation levels.

Table 5.1 2015 Funding Scenarios Using HEPI

State	2000 Appropriation Actual	2015 Appropriation Projections Baseline	2015 Appropriation Projections Baseline Plus	2015 Appropriation Projections Benchmark
Arkansas	$605,439,000	$1,125,823,477	$1,350,988,173	$2,104,407,047
California	$7,683,934,000	$17,467,304,723	$20,960,765,667	$20,589,773,941
Idaho	$279,290,000	$589,038,190	$706,845,828	$886,713,820
Michigan	$2,073,579,000	$3,744,363,150	$4,493,235,780	$5,036,396,559
New York	$3,126,582,000	$5,860,435,181	$7,032,522,217	$7,402,764,680

Three important points provide some perspective when viewing the magnitude of the increases shown in the different scenarios. First, the differences in funding between any state scenario and the 2000 appropriation are over the course of 15 years. This means that 15 years' worth of inflation is factored into the projections. The inflation factor of 77.7 percent used to calculate the funding projections for all three scenarios reflects the financial concept of compounding. The compounding effect is an inherent property of inflation. Compounding means each year's appropriation increase, due to inflation, becomes a permanent part of next year's appropriation. Thus, the effect of compounding is cumulative over time. For example, if 4 percent inflation is added to this year's appropriation of $100, then next year's base appropriation will be $104. The new inflation assumption will then be factored into the $104 dollars to determine subsequent appropriations. The 77.7 percent inflation factor used to project the 2015 appropriations in Table 5.1 and Appendix K really represents a compounded annual inflation rate of 3.9 percent, which is slightly less than the 4.0 percent average annual growth rate.[11]

The enrollment growth between 2000 and 2015 is also reflected in the funding increases shown in Table 5.1 and Appendix K. Enrollment growth is not compounded and is not cumulative. Most students do not stay enrolled in higher education forever; some students leave while other students enroll. The growth in enrollment from 2000 to 2015 represents the actual percentage difference in enrollment between the two time periods. According to the enrollment projections from Chapters 3 and 4, every state will experience enrollment increases for every scenario.

The percentage funding increases associated with the three scenarios are shown in Table 5.2 as a complement to Table 5.1. The percentage increase for each scenario is calculated relative to 2000 appropriations, so the percentage change is for the 15-year period between 2000 and 2015. The last column in the table shows the historical change in state appropriations between 1985 and 2000 as a basis for comparison with each scenario. The historical figures were calculated from the Grapevine.[12] Appendix L shows the appropriation increases from 2000 to 2015 for all 50 states. Appendix L also shows the appropriation increases from 1985 to 2000 for all 50 states.

The last column in Table 5.2 provides some perspective on the magnitude of the funding increases that happened over the past 15 years as compared to the projected funding changes for the three future scenarios. Arkansas, Idaho, and Michigan have over the past 15 years increased funding on a percentage basis more than or equal to the percentage

Table 5.2 2015 Funding Scenario Increases

State	Appropriation Increases: 2000–2015			Appropriation Increase: 1985–2000
	Baseline	Baseline Plus	Benchmark	
Arkansas	86.0%	123.1%	247.6%	102.3%
California	127.3%	172.8%	168.0%	83.3%
Idaho	110.9%	153.1%	217.5%	129.2%
Michigan	80.6%	116.7%	142.9%	80.9%
New York	87.4%	124.9%	136.8%	22.8%

increases necessary to meet baseline funding needs over the next 15 years. No state in the table has increased funding at a historical rate that equals or surpasses the percentage increases necessary to meet baseline plus or benchmark funding needs, according to Table 5.2.

The 15-year increase from 1985 to 2000 is the actual percentage funding increase that states provided to higher education. This statistic says nothing of what states in 1985 should have expected to provide if they would have projected 15 years forward. The historical appropriation increases shown in Table 5.2 do provide a reference point for comparison with the coming 15-year period, but they do not answer the question as to whether a state's historical funding met expectations.

If a state has met funding expectations in the past, then absent any other information, it can be assumed that it will meet funding expectations in the future. One way to gauge whether a state's actual 2000 appropriation met expectations is to use the 1985 appropriation (15 years past) to calculate what the expected 2000 appropriation should have been, based on certain criteria. For consistency, the criteria to calculate the expected appropriation for 2000 should be the same criteria used to calculate future funding projections for 2015: enrollment growth and inflation. Past enrollments for 1985 and 2000 are available from the U.S. Department of Education (NCES, 2001b), so the 15-year changes in enrollment for this time period can be calculated easily. This growth can be applied to the 1985 appropriations to predict what appropriations states might have expected in 2000 based on changes in enrollments.

Inflation growth from 1985 to 2000 is also known. The inflation assumption used to project future funding was based on the actual 15-year history of the HEPI. This inflation factor represents the actual rise

Table 5.3 Comparison of 2000 Expected and Actual Appropriations

State	Expected 2000 Appropriation	Actual 2000 Appropriation	Percentage Difference
Arkansas	$784,997,548	$605,439,000	−29.7%
California	$9,106,403,134	$7,683,934,000	−18.5%
Idaho	$328,095,010	$279,290,000	−17.5%
Michigan	$2,243,936,407	$2,073,579,000	−8.2%
New York	$4,617,934,114	$3,126,582,000	−47.7%

in prices in higher education, as measured by HEPI, between 1985 and 2000. This actual 77.7 percent increase can be used to estimate what level of funding states might have expected to provide in 2000. With the actual increase in HEPI and the historical growth in enrollment between 1985 and 2000, it is possible to compare the expected 2000 and actual 2000 appropriation. States may then conclude if historical higher education funding met expectations based on inflation and enrollment.

Table 5.3 shows the expected and actual 2000 appropriation for the five sample states. The expected 2000 appropriation for each state was based on three factors: 1985 appropriation, inflationary increase, and enrollment change. The percentage difference between the expected and actual appropriation is shown in the last column of the table. Appendix M shows the funding projections for all 50 states.

After accounting for actual inflation and enrollment growth, no state in Table 5.3 met its expected appropriation level for 2000. Of the five states in the table, Michigan was the closest to meeting its expected 2000 appropriation while New York was furthest from meeting its expected appropriation. Michigan's actual 80.9 percent appropriation increase from 1985 to 2000 (Table 5.2) was, by comparison, well maintained considering that the HEPI accounts for 77.7 percent of the expected increase and enrollment only grew 10.2 percent. New York, on the other hand, had a modest 2.1 percent enrollment growth during this time period, but the 22.8 percent appropriation increase during this time period did not even cover the inflation increase.

Table 5.3 does presume that in 1985 states correctly predicted inflation increases and 2000 enrollments. If a state estimated inflation or enrollment below what actually happened, then its expected appropriation would have been lower as well. If a state estimated inflation or enrollment above what actually happened, then its expected appropriation would have been higher than what is shown in Table 5.3.

Four of the five states in Tables 5.3 increased their appropriations beyond the 77.7 percent growth in inflation for the 1985 to 2000 time period. Most of the states, according to Appendix M, increased appropriations beyond the growth in inflation but still remained below the expected appropriation level. One interpretation for the states represented in Table 5.3 and Appendix M is that most increased appropriations from 1985 to 2000 to account for either inflation or enrollment increases or only a portion of each.

Conclusion

The issue of higher education finance is always a delicate topic that has a degree of subjectivity. Different stakeholders hold honest differences about how money should be appropriated, where it should be appropriated, and whether appropriated amounts are adequate. These issues are often the subject of much debate. Predictably, those outside higher education often feel that institutions get more than enough, while those inside the institutions feel that they do not have enough. Bowen's influential book, *The Costs of Higher Education,* outlined some important goals for higher education but offered five natural laws of higher education costs that remain controversial today (Bowen, 1980):

1. The dominant goals of institutions are educational excellence, prestige and influence.
2. In the quest for excellence, prestige, and influence, there is virtually no limit to the amount of money an institution could spend for seemingly fruitful ends.
3. Each institution raises all the money it can.
4. Each institution spends all it raises.
5. The cumulative effect of the preceding four laws is toward ever increasing expenditures.

Bowen has arguably been the most articulate voice for promoting the public and private benefits of higher education over the years. Yet, Bowen's laws of higher education cost have a bit of sting to them—especially for those who work in higher education. Bowen's work on the benefits of higher education is a constant reminder that the state has a responsibility to adequately fund higher education; his laws are the countervailing balance that suggests higher education must wisely steward the public monies it receives. Hovey's (1999) work on state spending is a reminder to any state agency that sensitivity to cost is important because it will have to battle just to sustain its future funding. From a policymaker's perspective, that battle exists because of the pressing needs from the multiple state agencies that compete for resources.

The work in this chapter outlined the funding parameters needed to maintain current service levels for those who will seek access in the future. It is a starting point to simultaneously think about access, costs, and benefits. In short, the funding projections only provide a view of resources that may be needed in the future. This view is not intended to be exact, because factors such as efficiency, student choice, and funding methodologies cannot possibly be integrated into the projections. Importantly, however, is that the future decisions that policymakers do control will influence cost—and access. Chapter 6 explores the effect of different higher education policies on institutions and students in the context of future demographic changes.

CHAPTER 6

State Policy and Higher Education Supply

In 2015, population growth across the states will push the demand for higher education to record levels. Nationally, an additional 1.2 million 18- to 24-year-olds will enroll in postsecondary education, assuming that states maintain their current participation rates.[13] Over 1 million additional people 25 and older will seek postsecondary education and training, pushing the total for this age group past 9.2 million nationwide.[14] If state policies encourage participation and improve participation rates across both age groups, enrollments will grow even more.

There is little doubt that more Americans are going to want access to higher education in the future. The future growth in the demand for higher education will continue a historical trend that Heller (2001b) recently tracked. Heller found that for nearly 30 years, the price of higher education continued to rise faster than the rate of inflation, yet enrollments also rose. Economically, rising prices tend to blunt demand, yet the rise in higher education enrollments from 1971 through 1998 clearly contradicted this theoretical expectation. Heller's explanation for why enrollments continued to climb in the face of price increases was attributed to a combination of economic and social factors that effectively changed the nature of the demand for higher education:

1. A growing wage premium for college graduates;
2. Affirmative action; and
3. Increased labor force participation by women and minorities.

These forces will continue into the future. The lifetime earnings differential between those who receive a college education and those who do not will continue to fuel demand. There may be more legal challenges to affirmative action in the future, but the Supreme Court's ruling on June 23, 2003, assured that the policy will continue for some time (*Gratz v. Bollinger*, 2003). The number of minorities on our nation's campuses can be expected to increase, although the percentage of minorities who have access to higher education will not necessarily increase. Finally, the growth (in absolute numbers) of women and minorities on college campuses means that the labor force will continue to diversify. As these forces converge to encourage higher education demand, so too will the sheer power of demographic growth.

State policy can also affect the demand for higher education. It might be argued, for instance, that by providing need-based financial aid, states broaden access by increasing opportunities for potential students. This, in effect, changes the demand for higher education. Just as state policy affects the demand for higher education, it also affects the supply of higher education. Supply speaks to the availability of higher education services in a state. Institutions are the providers of these services, and their capacity to offer higher education services is influenced by state policy. Supply is the opposite side of the demand coin.

State policy influences the supply of higher education in many ways. States directly influence the supply of higher education services by the level of funding they provide to institutions. Most states are also involved, to some extent, in the governance of institutions, and the type and number of institutions that exist. Any state policy aimed at the funding, governance, or operations of institutions influences supply. Students are ultimately affected by these policies, just as institutions are affected by policies directed toward students.

The influence of state policy on the supply of public higher education cannot be underestimated. Public institutions account for 77 percent of the higher education population,[15] and many states also work with private institutions to fulfill public purposes. In 2015, states will have to do little to increase the demand for higher education but a lot to accommodate it. Successful states will accommodate the coming demand by implementing state policy that speaks to both supply and demand. Policymakers have expressed their desire to increase access to higher education while maintaining what they term "affordability" (Ruppert, 2001). As the two scenarios in Figure 6.1 show, it is possible to maintain price and maximize access by shifting supply (through policy) to meet the coming shifts in demand. Each scenario displays the supply and demand for higher education for 2000 and 2015. The sup-

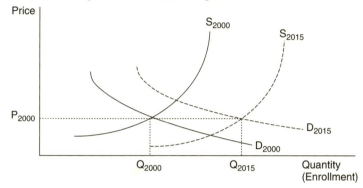

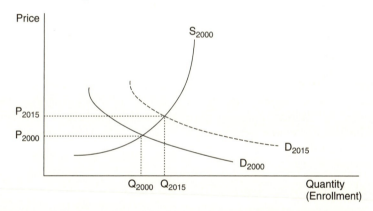

Figure 6.1 Two scenarios of higher education supply and demand in 2015.

ply and demand are graphed along two axes: price and quantity. In the case of higher education, price is the tuition that students pay, and quantity is the number of students enrolled.

In each scenario, the dotted curves represent future supply and demand in 2015. The solid curves represent 2000 supply and demand. In Scenario 1, curve S_{2000} and curve D_{2000} represent the 2000 supply and demand for higher education. Social, political, economic, and demographic changes will result in the outward shift of the demand curve in 2015 as described in Chapters 3 and 4 and as shown by curve D_{2015}. In this scenario, states keep prices at the same level, in constant dollar terms, by successful policy interventions that move the supply curve in 2015 to S_{2015}. In Scenario 1, the 2000 prices (P_{2000}) are maintained in 2015 and the future demand for higher education is at the enrollment level of Q_{2015}. A successful intervention is defined as any policy that shifts the supply curve in such a way that it maintains the 2000 price level, given the new demand curve D_{2015}. Examples of policy options that shift the supply curve outward are the subject of the next section.

In Scenario 2, curve S_{2000} and curve D_{2000} again represent the 2000 supply and demand for higher education. Social, political, economic, and demographic changes will result in the outward shift of the demand curve in 2015, as shown by curve D_{2015}. In this scenario, the price for higher education rises above the constant 2000 level. State policy is absent or ineffective, and the result is that the supply curve for 2015 stays in the same place as in 2000. In Scenario 2, the enrollment level of Q_{2015} is higher than the Q_{2000} level but lower than the 2015 enrollment level in Scenario 1. Heller's explanation of continued demand, even in the face of price increases, will certainly continue, but the level of enrollment increases in the future will be limited without effective state policy. In effect, rising prices in Scenario 2 do not decrease demand but rather limit actual enrollment. The next section discusses options for how states might increase supply and manage prices. These options include but extend beyond simply increasing state appropriations for higher education.

Successful State Policy in the Future

Given the near certainty that the demand for higher education is going to increase, policymakers will have to do little to encourage overall demand in their states. The issue that policymakers will have to address on the demand side of the higher education equation will have more to do with *who* has access to higher education. Is future enrollment going to be reflective of the income, age, and racial/ethnic diversity reflected in the states? What will be the mix of merit and need-based financial aid in the future? How will states keep their best and the brightest while giving every motivated individual the chance for a college education, regardless of race or income? Will states include policies that encourage the adult student population to attend college? The answers to such questions will address the details of future higher education demand. States will have to concern themselves with options to answer such questions, but the overall demand across the states will continue to rise.

The key to maintaining price and meeting future demand is also dependent on the availability of state higher education capacity and service delivery. Capacity and delivery are issues of supply. If, as documented, forces tend to shift higher education demand outward, prices (tuition) will tend to rise. Price increases can be moderated if state policy shifts the supply curve outward as well, as shown in Scenario 1, Figure 6.1. Such a shift will increase supply, maximize enrollment, and preserve price. Policies that can potentially shift the supply curve outward should be aimed at: (1) the number and type of higher education institutions, (2) improving efficiencies within higher education, (3) technology, or (4) institutional appropriations.

Changes in the Number and Type of Higher Education Institutions

States differ in terms of the number and type of higher education institutions that serve their populations. California's 1960 Master Plan very purposely distinguished three tiers for the higher education system: the California Community College system, the California State University system, and the University of California. Today, the state's massive community college system accommodates more enrollment than any other system in the state. The role of the two-year sector in other states is quite limited, with enrollments concentrated in four-year institutions. Kane and Rouse (1999) found that states with developed community college systems tend to have less-developed four-year systems, and states with developed four-year systems tend to have less-developed two-year systems.

The mix of public and private institutions also varies across states. Private institutions are integral to higher education systems in the northeastern United States, whereas their presence in many western states is limited. For example, the majority of undergraduate students in New Hampshire, New York, Massachusetts, and Pennsylvania attend private four-year institutions.[16] Some states with substantial private sectors actually buy services from private institutions or provide money for enrollments. In New Jersey, private four-year institutions receive state-operating dollars based on an enrollment-driven formula (Richardson, 2002)—though appropriations for public four-year institutions do not work in the same manner.

Higher education capacity is an issue of supply. Two- and four-year institutions that fully utilize all of their resources for the current level of enrollment operate at full capacity. These institutions do not have any additional supply. States that are at full capacity can increase the supply of higher education by building additional infrastructure at two- or four-year institutions or building new campuses. Institutions that are able to enroll additional students without increasing their resources have unused capacity. Institutions with unused capacity may already have adequate supply to meet future demand.

In many states, deliberate policy action has influenced growth in a particular sector. Public policy can build capacity in a particular sector to encourage enrollment in that sector. The state of Washington has long encouraged its students to begin in public two-year institutions. Today, community colleges in Washington account for the majority of higher education enrollments.

Over the last 20 years, enrollments throughout the United States have shifted by sector and level. It is impossible to determine whether these cumulative shifts have been the result of state policy that has influenced supply or demographic patterns that have influenced demand. In actuality, it is probably a combination of the two. In 1979, the public four-year sector accounted for 43 percent of all postsecondary enrollments in the nation but dropped to 40.5 percent by 1999. The gains were primarily made by the public two-year sector, which increased from 35.1 percent to 36.3 percent, and the private four-year sector, which increased from 20.5 percent to 21.5 percent during the same time period.[17]

In the future, states may wish to align their capacity-building efforts with projected demographic patterns. States expecting large population increases in the 18- to 24-year-old population may focus their efforts at different institutions than those expecting large population increases in the 25 and older population. Historically, community colleges have been regarded as accommodating to the 25 and over population. Kane and Rouse (1999, p. 86) reported that 36 percent of community college students are at least 30 years old, compared to only 22 percent of public four-year college students. Students at four-year institutions are older today than in the past, but the four-year sector continues to serve a larger percentage of traditional students than the two-year sector. A perhaps surprising result is shown in Figure 6.2. Nationally, this figure shows that the majority of students on two-year campuses are now in the 18- to 24-year-old age group.

Community colleges still serve a large percentage of students 25 and older and will continue to do so. Almost 80 percent of these students are enrolled part time.[18] The growth of the traditional student population in community colleges does raise an important policy question: Should states build capacity at two-year institutions and encourage stu-

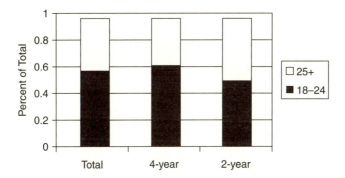

Figure 6.2 Fall enrollment by age and level. (*Source: Author's calculations. NCES, Fall Enrollment in Degree Granting Institutions, 1999, Table 176. Totals may not add to 100 percent due to students under 18 and those counted whose age is "unknown."*)

dents from both age groups to start at the community college? From a state perspective, it is cost efficient for students to start at a community college, even if their intention is to transfer to a more expensive four-year university for their last two years of study. The real savings states might achieve by encouraging students to start at a community college are somewhat tempered by the limited number of such students who actually persist and obtain a terminal degree. Kane and Rouse (1999) found that of those starting in two-year colleges, less than 16 percent complete at least a bachelor's degree and over 53 percent don't complete a certificate or any type of degree. Degree completion for those who start out in a four-year college is much higher. These statistics could be a point of contention in some states if lower income and minority students are encouraged to attend community colleges when they are already disproportionately represented in them.

Some states may choose to focus resources on a certain age group or sector based on future demographic trends. The issue of resource emphasis by age group assumes that states would be able to effectively channel resources to benefit a certain age group. There is some evidence that policy decisions sometimes benefit a certain age group or higher education sector, whether intended or unintended. In 1997, for example, New Mexico instituted a state lottery scholarship program, which benefits high school graduates. The New Mexico Commission on Higher Education's goal of encouraging student entry in the community colleges was somewhat circumvented by the availability of the lottery scholarships (Martinez, 2002). Students who may have first entered into a community college—or not enrolled in any college—suddenly considered the university a legitimate option with the emergence of the scholarship program. The lottery scholarships cover the full cost of tuition at either public two- or four-year institutions, effectively eliminating any price differentials between institutions.

According to enrollment data, university enrollment growth coincided with the commencement and continuation of the lottery scholarship program (Martinez, M.C. 2002). Given the dramatic projected growth of the 25 and older population in New Mexico, the state may wish to consider alternative options that intentionally include opportunities for the adult student population. One possibility is to make sure that two-year institutions have enough capacity to accommodate projected enrollment increases in the 25+ population. Another possibility is to create financial incentives that target this age group, making college at either the two- or four-year institutions more affordable.

The state of Nevada is similar to New Mexico in that the 25+ population will become a bigger proportion of the 18 and older population in 2015, but the best higher education policies for New Mexico may not be effective in Nevada. In Nevada, the average student age at four-year institutions is quite high. For this reason, four-year institutions may require additional capacity in the future. The state is also in need of policy options to encourage students to attend postsecondary education immediately after high school. Even though both Nevada and New Mexico will see a surge in the 25+ student population, their strategies for increasing access will likely differ.

There are many states that will see proportional increases in their 18- to 24-year-old populations in 2015. California and New York's traditional student enrollments will grow at a faster rate than their 25+ age group enrollments. The 18- to 24-year-old comparison ratios for California and New York show that in 2015 the participation rates in these states will lose ground relative to the national average if they only maintain their current participation rates. Policymakers in California and New York may wish to focus their efforts on state policies that boost 18- to 24-year-old participation rates above their current levels. One reaction may be to target resources to the four-year institutions since they have traditionally met the majority of the 18- to 24-year-old enrollment demand. Alternatively, California and New York may be highly motivated to encourage 18- to 24-year-olds to enter postsecondary education through the community college's doors since that is more cost efficient.

The issue of institutional mix will be prominent in states with shifting age group demographics. There are potential costs and benefits to any policy that modifies the institutional mix in its postsecondary industry. The best that can be said is that the trade-offs inherent in any prospective state policy change should be identified so that an informed discourse may emerge. The resulting policy should be based on a mixture of values, ideals, and fiscal realities unique to the state. No state would be advised to completely ignore one sector over the other simply because of demographic shifts in the population. A focus on either the two- or four-year sector does not imply the exclusion of policy in the other sector.

Economies of Scale: Achieving Operational Efficiencies

Efficient operations mean more service can be produced with the same amount of resources. In higher education, this would mean that more students could be educated with the same amount of resources. Economies of scale suggest that each additional student could be educated for less cost than the previous student. There is a point where additional resources (instructors, classrooms, laboratories, parking lots, etc.) are needed because the institution is operating at maximum efficiency and it has no more capacity. Economies of scale no longer apply after this point. More students beyond this point, without additional resources, mean lower quality in the delivery of higher education services.

The issue of efficiency is constantly debated in state higher education policy. Institutions that raise tuition when state appropriations are cut are implicitly signaling their belief that they are operating efficiently. The only way to maintain quality services is to increase prices to make up for lost state funding. Those who argue against tuition increases in spite of appropriation decreases are signaling their belief that higher education is not operating as efficiently as possible.

The various parties involved in higher education policy will continue to debate over the enrollment level where economies of scale no longer apply. The one constant in this debate is that efficiency is linked to supply. Increased efficiency means more supply, and more supply can meet increased demand while moderating price increases to the student. Improved efficiency is important because it is one way to move the supply curve outward, as shown in Figure 6.1, Scenario 1. In the parlance of higher education, this means that more students can be educated with existing resources without increasing tuition. Economists would describe a shift in the supply curve caused by improved efficiency as a change in the cost of production.

Accountability

The dominant policy mechanism states have used to ensure efficient operations within higher education is accountability. Monitoring and assessment systems are commonplace in states across the nation today, and it can be expected that such systems will continue to evolve. The external pressures on higher education to become more accountable have been generated by the reality of limited state resources, rising educational costs, the need for highly skilled workers, and the demand for equity and access to educational programs and services. Albright (1998) found that 32 states use or planned to use performance indicators. A study by Burke and Serban (1997) reported that states used varying numbers of performance indicators, from as many as 37 to as few as 9.

If accountability systems produce greater efficiencies, then states will increase their supply of higher education and have more capacity to meet future demand. A state's ability to collect and analyze information is dependent on the sophistication of its technological infrastructure and its system of governance. The technological capability to handle accountability is often lacking and requires significant investment. In 1995, the state of South Carolina began to move in the direction of performance-based funding. The state, at the time, passed Act 359, which mandated that future funding of public higher education be based on 37 indicators, not on the enrollment-driven formula of the past (Trombley, 1999). Ambitious initiatives like the past effort in South Carolina force states to assess their technological capability. The massive data collection and reporting requirements often necessitate updates and improvements to existing systems. If the resources for the updates and improvements are not available, the initiative will fall short of expectations. In the case of South Carolina, political conflict and the information technology infrastructure challenges certainly factored into the state's decision to back away from its aggressive plan to link funding to 37 indicators.

A state's ability to implement effective accountability systems is also tied to governance. States that lack a central state entity with sufficient resources or political influence have trouble collecting information to enhance accountability. In such an environment, state-level entities commonly lack links to institutional databases, which effectively leaves the state dependent on information that institutions or systems choose to provide. For instance, Michigan has no formal coordinating board to collect and analyze data. Consequently, policymakers in Michigan have few if any accountability mechanisms in place to ensure institutional accountability. California has a coordinating board, but resources are limited and the board often relies on the different systems to provide information. Michigan and California are examples of states that lack the governance systems or the technological capability to initiate the type of accountability systems that will be required as the competition for resources and the demand for higher education continue to climb.

Technology and Supply

Technology, insofar as it supports accountability efforts, indirectly affects the supply of higher education. Technology also directly affects supply. Technology expands the supply of education by enabling new or existing postsecondary providers to offer additional services. The expansion of educational services via technology can take many forms. Many colleges and universities across the United States are offering distance education courses in the form of interactive television or via the Internet. Public universities in states like North Carolina are offering distance education courses to serve rural areas that previously had limited access to postsecondary services. Britain's Open University, whose past enrollments number well over 200,000 distance students, represents an example of how operations in one location can create supply and meet demand in remote locations throughout a country or the world. It is not uncommon to find elite American universities offering MBA degrees in multiple states and countries via technology. All of these examples represent a new supply of higher education services that are meeting and creating demand.

Technology as an agent of educational expansion increases the supply of higher education. This shift is distinguished from a shift in the supply due to efficiency gains. Oberlin (1996) firmly asserts that the total cost of owning and maintaining technology is constantly increasing, and the demand for new and better technology is growing faster than prices are falling. Higher education and state leaders have learned that technology requires significant upfront investment and ongoing maintenance and updating (Ruppert, 2001). Technology can create many solutions and take education to new places, but the argument that technology leads to significant savings and efficiency increases remains unresolved. Perhaps the main point is that technology has and is currently being used as a tool to expand supply of education, regardless of what the costs have been. Britain's Open University is just one of many examples of how educational organizations use technology to expand supply. The National Center for Educational Statistics (2003) stated that the use of technology has been increasing at the same time that participation in college programs and adult education has increased, leading to the logical possibility that technology could help increase participation.

Institutional Appropriations

Higher education has been susceptible to the boom and bust of state economies. In the early part of the 1990s, states disproportionately cut higher education spending in an effort to balance their budgets. In the latter half of the 1990s, states increased higher education appropriations by about 7 percent for three years in a row (Selingo, 2003). The supply of higher education services follows the feast or famine nature of higher education budgets. In the context of a growing demand for postsecondary education, institutions can use increased state appropriations to make services more widely available, which causes an outward shift in the supply curve (increases supply). As states decrease institutional appropriations, institutions often cut or reduce services, which causes an inward shift of the supply curve (reduces supply).

State appropriations that flow directly to institutions should be distinguished from state appropriations that flow to students in the form of student aid. State policy aimed at student aid influences demand, whereas policy aimed at institutions influences supply. Regardless of the differing state philosophies on student aid, every state provides direct funding to its institutions. It is the job of the policymaker to judge how much institutions should receive and what proportion of a state's appropriation should be in the form of institutional funding versus student aid. For better or worse, policymakers influence the supply side of the economic equation when they make decisions about institutional funding.

Conclusion

The future demand for higher education will increase, with little or no action from the states. For most states, demographic growth, the need for continuing education and retraining (Bailey & Mingle, 2003), and possible improvements in academic preparation are some of the more prominent factors that will contribute to the future demand for higher education. From the demand perspective, state policy should focus on ensuring access and equity for underrepresented and disadvantaged populations. McGuinness and Jones (2003) encourage state policymakers to consider county-level postsecondary data to ensure that state-level statistics do not mask disparities in educational opportunity among a state's subpopulations.

In the future, state policy will also influence whether the supply of higher education is sufficient to meet demand. States will have to examine their existing capacity to supply higher education and measure that against future demand. Policies aimed at capacity will adjust the number and type of institutions in a particular state in the future. Accountability is another state-level policy mechanism that states will continue to use in the future. The ideals of accountability expand supply by utilizing existing resources to the fullest extent possible. States will also be able to increase supply in the future if they are willing to invest in technology-related delivery systems that take education to new markets. This expansion may lead to long-run saving, or it may require continual maintenance and investment. Finally, state policy most obviously influences the supply of higher education through the funding that it provides to institutions. Institutions that use additional state funding to expand services or enroll more students effectively increase the supply of higher education.

State policy can and does influence the supply of postsecondary education. This influence can be intended and directional or haphazard and random. States that plan for the future will purposely implement policies to increase the supply of postsecondary education in a way that maximizes access for their populations while being sensitive to quality. At the same time, successful states will manage the details of future demand to ensure equity across their populations.

CHAPTER 7

Aligning Policymaker Expectations with Future Demand

The first section of this chapter draws heavily on two national surveys (Ruppert, 1996; Ruppert, 2001) that asked state legislators questions about postsecondary education. In the second section, enrollment projections are tied to the legislative input from the national surveys. Six states serve as minicase studies to consider the policy implications of the projections and surveys. The minicase studies were constructed for the purposes of this chapter and draw on analyses from the previous chapters.

Outcomes

Policymakers believe that higher education is linked to the economic, social, and cultural well-being of their states. Legislators are under pressure to show the results of their decisions, so it is no surprise that they frequently speak about the expectations they have of higher education. In two national surveys (Ruppert, 1996; Ruppert, 2001) that asked state legislators questions about postsecondary education, policymaker expectations were mostly focused on outcomes. Legislators outlined three main outcomes in Ruppert's (2001) most recent national survey:

1. Strengthen and diversify the economy;
2. Prepare and train a high-skill, high-wage workforce; and
3. Raise the level of educational attainment of the state's population.

The outcomes are connected to one another. A higher education system that successfully prepares a high-skill, high-wage workforce will raise educational attainment levels and strengthen the prospects for economic growth. The three outcomes place a strong emphasis on the economic benefits of higher education because state economies are important to legislators. Many legislators describe higher education as the economic engine of their state and equate quality higher education institutions with a strong and diversified economy. Legislators across the country associate the preparation and training of a high-skilled workforce in a "knowledge-based economy" with something more than a high school diploma.

The strong legislative focus on economics is partly explained by term limits. Many states now have term limits, which shorten the life span of policymakers and increase pressure on state lawmakers to show results. The public has also demonstrated a willingness to vote politicians out of office who are not perceived as producing immediate results. Economic growth, degree attainment, and starting salaries are measurable and provide policymakers with figures and statistics that they can attribute to their efforts.

The policymaker's focus on the economic benefits of higher education also matches what students emphasize. Astin's (1998) annual national freshmen survey has found a changing tide in what students want from higher education. Students in the 1960s thought that one of the most important reasons to attend college was to develop a meaningful philosophy of life. By the 1990s, the number-one reason students said attending college was important was to get a well-paying job.

Despite the converging forces that emphasize the economic benefits of higher education, policymakers do recognize the intangible value that individuals and society gain from higher levels of educational attainment. The focus on economic growth and individual salaries may be a product of the times. As the competition for state resources intensifies and the demand for higher education increases, it is a focus that will surely continue into the future.

Means and Ends

Legislators, for the most part, expressed reservations about becoming too involved in defining the activity (the means) that leads to the outcomes (the ends) they expect. At the same time, many policymakers believe effective management in certain areas leads to the specific outcomes they expect. In Ruppert's (2001) survey, respondents identified several areas that might be described as a legislative wish list of how higher education might become more responsive to the state:

- Efficiency: Better use of existing facilities to handle changing enrollment needs. Efficiency is important to state leaders, and they hope to achieve maximum usage of existing facilities and resources.
- Communication: More communication between two- and four-year institutions. Legislators view higher education as an important state agency but generally want to make sure that communication between institutions is taking place so that services are not unnecessarily duplicated and infighting is held to a minimum. Some legislators indicated that better communication could also enhance articulation between two- and four-year institutions, which in their view would be efficient and save the state money.
- Collaboration: Legislators increasingly refer to K–16 and "seamless" education when referencing their desire for K–12 and higher education to forge more partnerships. Legislators believe that collaboration between higher education and K–12 could improve student preparation and teacher quality.
- Affordability: Legislators expressed a desire to keep college affordable. They were concerned about rising tuition and generally believe access to a college education depends on affordable tuition prices.

Legislators connect efficiency, communication, collaboration, and affordability to a stronger economy, a qualified workforce, and increased levels of educational attainment. For example, legislators want to increase educational attainment in their states, but they believe more students can be educated if resources are utilized efficiently. From a state perspective, efficiency is also enhanced when institutions communicate. Communication may lead to cooperative agreements that strengthen articulation and transfer or forge partnerships so that students in one institution have access to courses in another.

Collaboration between higher education and K–12 is important since colleges produce the teachers who prepare students for life after high school. Qualified students are more likely to participate, persist, and obtain a degree. However, once students are prepared for postsecondary education and training, access must be available. State policymakers around the country use the terms "access" and "affordability" interchangeably. States have different perceptions about the mix of institutional funding and student aid that leads to affordability, but policymakers in general do convey a sense that the state has a responsibility to ensure affordability.

State policymakers will have different opinions as to how best to achieve any given outcome. The emphasis of and motivation for prioritizing one outcome over another will also differ by state. Despite nuances specific to each state, the legislative surveys provide a general sense of what is important to state policymakers. As state leaders look to the future, their policy priorities and the means to achieve them should in part be guided by the changing age group demographics of their states.

Changing Demographics and Higher Education Policy

Census data provide the age group population projections necessary to estimate future enrollment demand. Future enrollment projections can contribute to how higher education policy is shaped today. In turn, higher education policy should be guided by broad state goals. In this section, six states serve as minicase studies and outline some policy options that arise when demographic changes and broad state goals are compared against the state's current higher education environment. The minicase studies were constructed for the purposes of this chapter and draw on analyses from the previous chapters and other related standardized data sets. The minicases are necessarily abbreviated for illustration purposes. As such, the policy options that accompany each minicase primarily focus on the issues of capacity and efficiency as they relate to demographic changes in the states. There are undoubtedly additional policies that are just as important as capacity and efficiency. The minicases are only intended to be a springboard for conversation rather than a definition of comprehensive or absolute policy solutions for the states under study.

Case Study Examples

Many states across the nation will see a change in their age structure in the future. The six states in Table 7.1 show different patterns of age group shifts from 2000 to 2015. The role of the four-year sector and the proportion of 18- to 24-year-old enrollments are also very different across the six sample states. The six states represent a cross section of regions from around the country.

Table 7.1 shows statistics only for the 18- to 24-year-old population for the states. It is not necessary to show statistics for the 25+ population since they are implied from the 18- to 24-year-old statistics. For example,

Table 7.1 Demographics and Higher Education

State	Proportion of Adult Population: 18–24		18–24: Proportion of Enrollment	Proportion Enrolled in 4-Year Sector
	2000	2015	2000	2000
Colorado	13.4%	12.3%	47.1%	67.4%
Georgia	13.9%	13.4%	53.6%	75.8%
Massachusetts	11.9%	13.3%	54.3%	79.4%
North Dakota	15.1%	13.1%	68.2%	77.0%
Virginia	12.7%	12.8%	51.1%	62.2%
Washington	12.7%	11.7%	48.4%	42.8%
United States	12.9%	13.0%	52.9%	62.0%

in 2015, 18- to 24-year-olds will comprise 13 percent of the 18 and older population. This means that the remaining 87 percent (100 percent − 13 percent) of the 18 and older population will be 25 or older.

Table 7.1 is intended to be a starting point for the minicase discussions. The enrollment projections and additional characteristics that describe each state's higher education environment will also contribute to the minicases. Current and future statistics lead to policy options that legislators might consider useful as they try to reach the outcomes they deem important.

Colorado

The traditional student population is proportionally high in many states that have a majority of enrollment in four-year institutions. Colorado does not follow this pattern. Four-year institutions comprise over two-thirds of the state's enrollments, but 18- to 24-year-olds comprise less than half the postsecondary enrollment population. These patterns may be partly attributed to Colorado's higher than average percentage of professional and graduate student enrollment.[19]

In Colorado, the 18- to 24-year-old population will become a smaller proportion of the 18 and older population in 2015. This means that the 25 and older population will become a bigger proportion of the state population, though both age groups will grow in absolute terms. From Chapter 3, the baseline enrollment growth over 2000 levels will result in an additional demand of 26,564 students 25 and older and an additional 9,956 students from the 18- to 24-year-old age group.

The dynamics of the shifting age groups have several policy implications. First, it is safe to assume that only a portion of the additional demand from the 18 and older student population will be for graduate or professional education. If Colorado wishes to equip its two-year institutions to accommodate the 25+ population, then the state may consider additional capacity at this level. This, in turn, may mean only moderate capacity building at four-year institutions. It may also be possible that the existing two-year institutions are underutilized. If this is the case, then additional infrastructure would only be necessary after facility utilization has been maximized.

Capacity will become a prominent issue at both two- and four-year institutions if the state and institutions work to improve participation rates. Whether the state strives for baseline, baseline plus, or benchmark enrollment levels, there are indications that some emphasis on two-year institutions may help the state prepare for the growing 25 and older student population.

Georgia

The merit-based HOPE scholarship program that originated in Georgia in 1993 gained national attention and soon became a model for other states. Some state leaders in New Mexico believe that the merit-based lottery scholarship program in their state increased enrollments in the four-year institutions (Martinez, M.C. 2002), and Georgia's enrollment patterns may add credibility to that claim. Four-year institutions in Georgia account for 75.8 percent of the state's postsecondary enrollments, and 18- to 24-year-olds comprise more than half of the total student population. The shift in the 18 and older population will be modest, as 18- to 24-year-olds will represent 13.4 percent in 2015 as compared to 13.9 percent in 2000. The baseline enrollment growth over 2000 levels will result in an additional demand of 34,125 students 25 and older and an additional 28,958 students from the 18- to 24-year-old age group.

If the state builds additional capacity or increases efficiency at four-year institutions to accommodate the projected demand, the proportion of those enrolled at four-year institutions will likely approach 80 percent. The 2000 national average was 62 percent. Georgia may wish to encourage enrollment at two-year institutions, which presumably would serve the growing 25+ population. As in Colorado, additional capacity at the two-year level may be more cost effective and balance out the enrollment representation at the various two- and four-year institutions. Georgia may also have to consider different alternatives such as balancing enrollments between two- and four-year institutions if it is to keep the HOPE scholarship program fiscally solvent. Currently, a legislative-appointed task force is looking at projected shortfalls in HOPE funding. Although the future fiscal strategies to fund Georgia higher education are unknown, the state will continue to encourage four-year enrollments if it can find the money to support the institutions, the students, or both.

Massachusetts

No state in the nation utilizes the private four-year sector as much as Massachusetts, and no state has a higher proportion of its enrollment in four-year institutions, both public and private. Educational attainment and median income in Massachusetts are among the highest in the nation, as is the percentage of students who are enrolled in graduate programs. All of these factors help explain why the state enrolls a disproportionate percentage of students in four-year institutions—and there is no reason to expect significant changes given 2015 demographic projections. The proportion of 18- to 24-year-olds enrolled in higher education in the state is slightly higher than the national average, and that proportion will likely increase as 18- to 24-year-olds become a larger proportion of the 18 and older population in 2015.

From a policy perspective, it appears that Massachusetts must ensure continued capacity in its public four-year institutions to ensure access for its resident 18- to 24-year-old population. The state's efforts to maximize accessibility may need to focus on maintaining student tuition and fees at acceptable levels. If capacity is not added, student tuition and fees can be expected to skyrocket for two reasons: increased demand from 18- to 24-year-olds and limited space. From 1985 to 2000, the state's enrollment did not grow, but from 2000 to 2015, that situation will be very different given the projected population growth. The baseline enrollment growth over 2000 levels will result in an additional demand of 7,835 students 25 and older and an additional 44,831 students from the 18- to 24-year-old age group.

Massachusetts may consider another option to help accommodate its projected growth: utilize the private sector to a greater extent. The private sector in the state accounts for over half of the state's current enrollment. States such as New Jersey and Pennsylvania continue to use private-sector capacity to meet public needs, and an emphasis on similar strategies may be an important consideration for Massachusetts in the future.

North Dakota

North Dakota is successful at encouraging its residents to attend college in state while simultaneously attracting students from out of state.[20] North Dakota higher education statistics for 2000 heavily favor four-year institutions: 18- to 24-year-olds comprise a nation-leading 68.2 percent enrollment and four-year institutions account for 77 percent of the state's enrollment. The percentage of graduate and professional students is among the lowest in the nation. In short, North Dakota focuses on four-year undergraduate education for the traditional student population.

North Dakota may have to consider policy changes in the future, as its demographic shifts will lead to enrollment demand from students who desire services other than those that are currently emphasized. The 18- to 24-year-old population will become a smaller proportion of the 18 and older population, from 15.1 percent in 2000 to 13.1 percent in 2015. The absolute number of 18- to 24-year-olds in the 18 and older population will actually decrease over time. The 25 and older population will become a bigger proportion of the state population and will exert pressure on the state and its institutions to provide services to meet its needs. The projected baseline enrollment changes from 2000 levels will result in an additional demand of 2,145 students 25 and older and a decrease of 962 students from the 18- to 24-year-old age group.

If the state hopes to maintain its four-year undergraduate programs, it would have to channel more students 25 and older into the current system, further increase out-of-state enrollment, or a combination of the two. These strategies would make use of the capacity in the four-year institutions, which may not be fully utilized otherwise. Another option would be to build capacity or more fully utilize two-year institutions.

Virginia

Many of Virginia's demographic and postsecondary statistics are similar to composite averages for the nation. The enrollment proportion of 18- to 24-year-olds is 51.1 percent, compared to the national average of 52.9 percent; four-year institutions account for 62.2 percent of Virginia's student population, compared to the national average of 62 percent. As in Georgia, the shift in Virginia's 18 and older population will not be significant, as 18- to 24-year-olds will represent 12.8 percent in 2015 as compared to 12.7 percent in 2000. The baseline enrollment growth over 2000 levels will result in an additional demand of 33,579 students 25 and older and an additional 39,596 students from the 18- to 24-year-old age group.

Virginia utilizes its two- and four-year institutions, both public and private, quite well. The state's public two-year enrollments (36.1 percent) are virtually equal to the national average (36.3 percent), and it relies on public four-year institutions (46.4 percent) slightly more than the national average (40.5 percent).[21] The major policy decisions in the state may not lie in designing strategies to change the mix of institutions in the state but rather to fund them adequately enough to improve baseline participation rates.

Virginia's use of institutions is diverse and should be preserved to maintain its current balance between the two age group enrollments. If Virginia strives to reach baseline plus or benchmark participation rates, it may be necessary to build additional capacity that allows the state to do not only the same things but more of the same things.

Washington

Washington disproportionately depends on its two-year institutions to meet its postsecondary needs, as is evident from the relatively small proportion of enrollment in the four-year sector compared to the national average (Table 7.1). As in North Dakota, the percentage of graduate and professional students is among the lowest in the nation. The projected population and enrollment changes indicate that the state's reliance on two-year institutions may be intensified in the future. The shift in Washington's 18 and older population will result in a higher proportion of people 25 and older in 2015. The baseline enrollment growth over 2000 levels will result in an additional demand of 47,737 students 25 and older and an additional 24,954 students from the 18- to 24-year-old age group.

Educational attainment and income per capita in Washington are high. Like Colorado, the state appears to import a large number of people who have been educated somewhere else. Although Washington will need to continue to equip its two-year institutions to meet the coming demand, the state may wish to consider shifting some emphasis to the four-year institutions. Such a strategy may give students more access to four-year degrees and build on its below-average emphasis on graduate students.

Achieving Outcomes

Each minicase provides a sketch of current state higher education characteristics compared to estimates of future enrollment. Additional economic, political, and demographic information would more fully develop the minicases and provide more policy options. The value of the minicases is that they demonstrate how state-level demographic characteristics and trends can inform policy discussion. Any policy that results from such discussion should be tied to broad state priorities and the institutional actions that legislators believe lead to the priorities.

Policy Outcomes for the 18- to 24-Year-Old Population

In the legislative surveys, policymakers stressed the importance of K–16 collaboration to improve educational attainment and prepare a high-skill workforce. This collaboration will be important in states that wish to maintain or improve participation rates for an increasing 18- to 24-year-old population. Every state in Table 7.1 except North Dakota should expect an absolute increase in the number of 18- to 24-year-olds in their populations. This will increase the demand for postsecondary education from this age group. In Massachusetts and Virginia, the pace of 18- to 24-year-old enrollment growth will surpass that of the 25+ age group. K–16 collaboration will be critical in these states. Collaboration will also be important in states where college entry rates for resident high school students appear problematic. In Colorado and Washington, for example, Mortenson (2002) found that the chance of a high school graduate going to college is lower than the national average.

The demographic growth of the traditional student population in states like Massachusetts and Virginia will tend to encourage tuition increases. One policy challenge in these states will be to maintain affordability in the face of a guaranteed increase in demand. Legislators tie affordability to access and ultimately to workforce preparation and educational attainment.

As outlined in Chapter 6, there are multiple policies that may work toward maintaining affordability. Georgia has focused on demand through its merit-based student aid, although the state has had its share of critics with regard to the subpopulations who may not benefit from such a strategy. Other states may choose to focus on policies that increase the supply of higher education to moderate tuition increases. In any state, the key to increasing supply may include some combination of technological solutions, increased efficiencies, accountability, and additional institutional investment.

Policy Outcomes for the 25+ Population

The increase in the 25 and older population will fuel demand from the adult student population for reasons ranging from a desire for more education to retooling for a new career. In the lexicon of policymakers, states that meet the educational needs of the 25 and older population will build a qualified workforce that creates a diversified economy. In addition, states that successfully improve their participation rates among the 18- to 24-year-old populations will not necessarily alleviate the need for continued education and training as those populations age. Changing economies and emerging technologies continue to create the need for additional postsecondary education for a number of adults (Bailey & Mingle, 2003).

Every state in Table 7.1 should expect an absolute increase in the number of people 25 and older in their populations. This trend by itself will increase the demand for postsecondary education from this age group. In Colorado and Washington, the expected enrollment demand from the 25+ age group will be substantial when compared to current enrollment trends. Georgia and Virginia will also see relatively large increases in enrollment demand from this age group. North Dakota's expected 25+ enrollment for 2015, though small in comparison to other states, is large relative to its current enrollment for this age group. North Dakota will have to revisit its assumptions about which age group should be the focus of explicit higher education policy and where that group should receive its services.

There is little question that lawmakers feel that community colleges and vocational institutions are the most responsive of all postsecondary institutions when it comes to providing the training and development necessary to attract business and industry (Ruppert, 2001). In states like Colorado, North Dakota, and Washington, there will be pressure to provide education and training to the growing 25+ population. The two-year institutions in Washington may have the experience to meet the growing need, since they are well established and an integral part of postsecondary education in the state. In Washington's case, properly equipping two-year institutions for the future may simply require more resources to accommodate future growth. In Colorado and North Dakota, policy may be the tool to more strongly integrate two-year institutions and the 25+ population into the postsecondary equation.

Conclusion

The sample states in Table 7.1 demonstrate how demographic changes in the future bear on higher education policy and the outcomes important to policymakers. In some cases, the demographic "chips" will fall in alignment with the current postsecondary infrastructure. Massachusetts, Georgia, Virginia, and Washington all have strengths in areas that appear to be aligned with future demographic growth. The key in these states may be to build on their strengths and do more of the same things. However, these states will have to make some adjustments to higher education policy to maintain affordability or shift some emphasis to a particular sector. For instance, if Georgia wishes to expand opportunity for those 25 and older, it may need to consider implementing incentives for this age group as it has for the traditional student population. If Washington wishes to expand its graduate and professional programs, it may need to channel resources and students to its four-year institutions.

Demographic changes will increase the pressure in some states to develop policy that changes the higher education landscape. North Dakota and Colorado are examples of states that have previously emphasized four-year institutions, but the projected growth in the 25+ enrollment will be stronger than ever and outpace demand from the 18- to 24-year-old age group. Policy in these states will be difficult to implement because current practices will have to change to reach desirable outcomes.

Significant changes or minor policy adjustments both require action. No matter what the challenge, most states can expect to face funding constraints that will heighten the need for deliberate policy debate. It is only through informed debate that a state can best pursue appropriate strategies to expand access and achieve its goals. In the future, then, each state will take one of two paths. The first path is that of purposeful policy. In this path, states will proactively use demographic information as an input to help guide higher education policy discussions. Each state will also consider its unique context to develop state-level goals that give rise to meaningful policy. The second path is inaction, the policy vacuum. In these states, higher education policy that is developed will be reactionary, ad hoc, based solely on anecdote, and not connected to state-level goals.

While there is no way to predict the future perfectly, future projections and historical trends can inform higher education policy. This book is not about trying to convince policymakers and the public to blindly increase their investment in higher education or promote one foolproof policy to meet the challenges of the future. There are different avenues by which states can maintain or increase postsecondary participation, improve educational attainment, and strengthen their economies through a well-qualified workforce. Demographic and funding projections are simply a tool to help state leaders develop linkages between policy and higher education performance.

APPENDIX A

2000 Participation Statistics, with Participation Rates

	Participation		Age Group Population		Participation Rate	
	18–24	25+	18–24	25+	18–24	25+
Alabama	145,569	96,497	437,088	2,887,400	33.3%	3.3%
Alaska	10,921	21,193	56,869	379,556	19.2%	5.6%
Arizona	149,538	179,737	511,747	3,256,184	29.2%	5.5%
Arkansas	75,014	52,522	262,142	1,731,200	28.6%	3.0%
California	1,186,716	1,357,149	3,351,285	21,298,900	35.4%	6.4%
Colorado	132,917	149,044	427,839	2,776,632	31.1%	5.4%
Connecticut	103,425	100,124	270,374	2,295,617	38.3%	4.4%
Delaware	28,318	22,985	74,980	514,658	37.8%	4.5%
Florida	419,576	462,541	1,323,161	11,024,645	31.7%	4.2%
Georgia	233,081	201,805	834,714	5,185,965	27.9%	3.9%
Hawaii	37,309	42,017	114,735	802,477	32.5%	5.2%
Idaho	42,457	34,427	38,317	787,505	30.7%	4.4%
Illinois	420,002	386,352	1,206,393	7,973,671	34.8%	4.8%
Indiana	210,462	141,385	614,401	3,893,278	34.3%	3.6%
Iowa	119,413	67,346	298,134	1,895,856	40.1%	3.6%
Kansas	100,694	75,080	275,991	1,701,207	36.5%	4.4%
Kentucky	118,476	87,285	401,531	2,646,397	29.5%	3.3%
Louisiana	153,457	103,283	475,055	2,775,468	32.3%	3.7%
Maine	34,328	32,606	104,052	869,893	33.0%	3.7%
Maryland	162,502	190,277	447,472	3,495,595	36.3%	5.4%
Massachusetts	255,990	215,785	579,855	4,273,275	44.1%	5.0%
Michigan	341,047	293,160	929,908	6,415,941	36.7%	4.6%
Minnesota	169,048	126,357	468,595	3,164,345	36.1%	4.0%
Mississippi	97,904	54,476	312,737	1,757,517	31.3%	3.1%
Missouri	175,609	142,980	534,203	3,634,906	32.9%	3.9%
Montana	28,907	22,052	85,630	586,621	33.8%	3.8%
Nebraska	67,163	44,894	174,407	1,087,241	38.5%	4.1%
Nevada	39,825	58,324	178,350	1,310,176	22.3%	4.5%
New Hampshire	39,677	35,029	102,898	823,987	38.6%	4.3%
New Jersey	236,808	231,609	675,077	5,657,799	35.1%	4.1%
New Mexico	51,333	68,231	176,677	1,134,801	29.1%	6.0%
New York	695,917	597,896	1,759,730	12,542,536	39.5%	4.8%
North Carolina	248,809	211,450	805,002	5,282,994	30.9%	4.0%
North Dakota	32,047	14,919	72,716	408,585	44.1%	3.7%
Ohio	360,721	289,839	1,056,259	7,411,740	34.2%	3.9%
Oklahoma	113,663	88,866	357,217	2,203,173	31.8%	4.0%
Oregon	100,319	103,190	326,131	2,250,998	30.8%	4.6%
Pennsylvania	427,711	273,261	1,095,782	8,266,284	39.0%	3.3%
Rhode Island	50,717	33,118	106,237	694,573	47.7%	4.8%
South Carolina	126,236	89,596	406,909	2,596,010	31.0%	3.5%
South Dakota	26,912	15,926	77,759	474,359	34.6%	3.4%
Tennessee	163,975	122,582	547,119	3,744,928	30.0%	3.3%
Texas	628,903	567,760	2,186,997	12,790,893	28.8%	4.4%
Utah	116,505	69,167	318,446	1,197,892	36.6%	5.8%
Vermont	24,552	15,655	57,025	404,223	43.1%	3.9%

	Participation		Age Group Population		Participation Rate	
	18–24	25+	18–24	25+	18–24	25+
Virginia	229,674	219,735	676,117	4,666,574	34.0%	4.7%
Washington	172,215	183,898	556,834	3,827,507	30.9%	4.8%
West Virginia	57,368	34,782	172,988	1,233,581	33.2%	2.8%
Wisconsin	189,767	137,990	520,411	3,475,878	36.5%	4.0%
Wyoming	15,808	13,780	50,022	315,663	31.6%	4.4%
United States	9,169,305	8,179,962	26,994,318	181,827,104	34.0%	4.5%

APPENDIX B

2000 Participation Statistics, with Comparison Ratios

APPENDIX B: 2000 PARTICIPATION STATISTICS 107

	Proportion 18 and Older		Comparison Ratio*	
	18–24	25+	18–24	25+
Alabama	13.1%	86.9%	2.53	0.038
Alaska	13.0%	87.0%	1.47	0.064
Arizona	13.6%	86.4%	2.15	0.064
Arkansas	13.2%	86.8%	2.17	0.035
California	13.6%	86.4%	2.60	0.074
Colorado	13.4%	86.6%	2.33	0.062
Connecticut	10.5%	89.5%	3.63	0.049
Delaware	12.7%	87.3%	2.97	0.052
Florida	10.7%	89.3%	2.96	0.047
Georgia	13.9%	86.1%	2.01	0.045
Hawaii	12.5%	87.5%	2.60	0.059
Idaho	14.9%	85.1%	2.05	0.052
Illinois	13.1%	86.9%	2.65	0.055
Indiana	13.6%	86.4%	2.52	0.042
Iowa	13.6%	86.4%	2.95	0.042
Kansas	14.0%	86.0%	2.61	0.051
Kentucky	13.2%	86.8%	2.24	0.038
Louisiana	14.6%	85.4%	2.21	0.043
Maine	10.7%	89.3%	3.09	0.041
Maryland	11.3%	88.7%	3.20	0.061
Massachusetts	11.9%	88.1%	3.69	0.057
Michigan	12.7%	87.3%	2.90	0.053
Minnesota	12.9%	87.1%	2.80	0.046
Mississippi	15.1%	84.9%	2.07	0.037
Missouri	12.8%	87.2%	2.57	0.045
Montana	12.7%	87.3%	2.65	0.044
Nebraska	13.8%	86.2%	2.79	0.048
Nevada	12.0%	88.0%	1.86	0.051
New Hampshire	11.1%	88.9%	3.48	0.048
New Jersey	10.7%	89.3%	3.29	0.046
New Mexico	13.5%	86.5%	2.16	0.069
New York	12.3%	87.7%	3.21	0.055
North Carolina	13.2%	86.8%	2.34	0.046
North Dakota	15.1%	84.9%	2.92	0.044
Ohio	12.5%	87.5%	2.74	0.045
Oklahoma	14.0%	86.0%	2.28	0.046
Oregon	12.7%	87.3%	2.43	0.053
Pennsylvania	11.7%	88.3%	3.33	0.037
Rhode Island	13.3%	86.7%	3.60	0.055
South Carolina	13.6%	86.4%	2.29	0.040
South Dakota	14.1%	85.9%	2.46	0.040
Tennessee	12.7%	87.3%	2.35	0.038
Texas	14.6%	85.4%	1.97	0.052
Utah	21.0%	79.0%	1.74	0.073
Vermont	12.4%	87.6%	3.49	0.045

	Proportion 18 and Older		Comparison Ratio*	
	18–24	25+	18–24	25+
Virginia	12.7%	87.3%	2.69	0.054
Washington	12.7%	87.3%	2.43	0.055
West Virginia	12.3%	87.7%	2.70	0.032
Wisconsin	13.0%	87.0%	2.80	0.046
Wyoming	13.7%	86.3%	2.31	0.051
United States	12.9%	87.1%	2.63	0.052

*Comparison Ratio = Participation Rate by Age Group/Age Group Proportion

Appendix C
2015 Population Statistics

	Absolute Population			% Change: 2000–2015		
	18–24	25+	18+	18–24	25+	18+
Alabama	474,222	3,374,347	3,848,569	8.5%	16.9%	15.8%
Alaska	87,809	461,376	549,185	54.4%	21.6%	25.8%
Arizona	564,818	3,811,592	4,376,410	10.4%	17.1%	16.1%
Arkansas	249,447	2,045,958	2,295,405	−4.8%	18.2%	15.2%
California	4,718,293	24,848,269	29,566,562	40.8%	16.7%	19.9%
Colorado	459,887	3,271,505	3,731,392	7.5%	17.8%	16.4%
Connecticut	327,511	2,393,574	2,721,085	21.1%	4.3%	6.0%
Delaware	80,660	566,881	647,541	7.6%	10.1%	9.8%
Florida	1,537,390	13,287,090	14,824,480	16.2%	20.5%	20.1%
Georgia	938,418	6,062,909	7,001,327	12.4%	16.9%	16.3%
Hawaii	156,012	988,516	1,144,528	36.0%	23.2%	24.8%
Idaho	145,439	1,066,044	1,211,483	5.1%	35.4%	30.9%
Illinois	1,287,962	8,336,130	9,624,092	6.8%	4.5%	4.8%
Indiana	614,658	4,305,442	4,920,100	0.0%	10.6%	9.1%
Iowa	267,436	2,053,452	2,320,888	−10.3%	8.3%	5.8%
Kansas	284,748	1,935,932	2,220,680	3.2%	13.8%	12.3%
Kentucky	384,071	2,944,880	3,328,951	−4.3%	11.3%	9.2%
Louisiana	502,218	3,113,128	3,615,346	5.7%	12.2%	11.2%
Maine	108,451	970,417	1,078,868	4.2%	11.6%	10.8%
Maryland	564,931	3,935,258	4,500,189	26.2%	12.6%	14.1%
Massachusetts	681,404	4,428,433	5,109,837	17.5%	3.6%	5.3%
Michigan	936,107	6,590,137	7,526,244	0.7%	2.7%	2.5%
Minnesota	476,195	3,574,795	4,050,990	1.6%	13.0%	11.5%
Mississippi	294,203	2,003,816	2,298,019	−5.9%	14.0%	11.0%
Missouri	555,426	4,063,145	4,618,571	4.0%	11.8%	10.8%
Montana	84,416	741,511	825,927	−1.4%	26.4%	22.9%
Nebraska	173,088	1,227,544	1,400,632	−0.8%	12.9%	11.0%
Nevada	187,216	1,536,078	1,723,294	5.0%	17.2%	15.8%
New Hampshire	122,551	945,871	1,068,422	19.1%	14.8%	15.3%
New Jersey	818,485	6,060,781	6,879,266	21.2%	7.1%	8.6%
New Mexico	220,384	1,451,741	1,672,125	24.7%	27.9%	27.5%
New York	1,958,481	12,379,977	14,338,458	11.3%	−1.3%	0.3%
North Carolina	839,033	6,124,822	6,963,855	4.2%	15.9%	14.4%
North Dakota	70,533	467,330	537,863	−3.0%	14.4%	11.8%
Ohio	1,083,205	7,825,515	8,908,720	2.6%	5.6%	5.2%
Oklahoma	358,398	2,554,359	2,912,757	0.3%	15.9%	13.8%
Oregon	333,613	2,807,812	3,141,425	2.3%	24.7%	21.9%
Pennsylvania	1,116,862	8,593,689	9,710,551	1.9%	4.0%	3.7%
Rhode Island	108,156	714,360	822,516	1.8%	2.8%	2.7%
South Carolina	416,822	2,978,624	3,395,446	2.4%	14.7%	13.1%
South Dakota	75,320	554,289	629,609	−3.1%	16.9%	14.0%
Tennessee	598,780	4,379,011	4,977,791	9.4%	16.9%	16.0%
Texas	2,639,950	15,113,145	17,753,095	20.7%	18.2%	18.5%
Utah	317,042	1,558,634	1,875,676	−0.4%	30.1%	23.7%
Vermont	59,151	458,153	517,304	3.7%	13.3%	12.2%

	Absolute Population			% Change: 2000–2015		
	18–24	25+	18+	18–24	25+	18+
Virginia	792,680	5,379,706	6,172,386	17.2%	15.3%	15.5%
Washington	637,519	4,821,063	5,458,582	14.5%	26.0%	24.5%
West Virginia	153,473	1,333,598	1,487,071	−11.3%	8.1%	5.7%
Wisconsin	513,632	3,865,562	4,379,194	−1.3%	11.2%	9.6%
Wyoming	58,388	422,277	480,665	16.7%	33.8%	31.4%
United States	30,515,711	205,095,143	235,610,854	13.0%	12.8%	12.8%

APPENDIX D

2015 Participation Statistics

APPENDIX D: 2015 PARTICIPATION STATISTICS

	Age Group Proportion		Baseline Enrollment		
	18–24	25+	18–24	25+	18+
Alabama	12.3%	87.7%	157,936	112,771	270,707
Alaska	16.0%	84.0%	16,863	25,762	42,624
Arizona	12.9%	87.1%	165,046	210,395	375,441
Arkansas	10.9%	89.1%	71,381	62,071	133,453
California	16.0%	84.0%	1,670,784	1,583,312	3,254,096
Colorado	12.3%	87.7%	142,873	175,608	318,481
Connecticut	12.0%	88.0%	125,281	104,396	229,678
Delaware	12.5%	87.5%	30,463	25,317	55,781
Florida	10.4%	89.6%	487,508	557,462	1,044,971
Georgia	13.4%	86.6%	262,039	235,930	497,969
Hawaii	13.6%	86.4%	50,731	51,758	102,489
Idaho	12.0%	88.0%	44,643	46,604	91,247
Illinois	13.4%	86.6%	448,400	403,914	852,314
Indiana	12.5%	87.5%	210,550	156,353	366,903
Iowa	11.5%	88.5%	107,117	72,944	180,062
Kansas	12.8%	87.2%	103,889	85,439	189,328
Kentucky	11.5%	88.5%	113,324	97,130	210,454
Louisiana	13.9%	86.1%	162,231	115,848	278,080
Maine	10.1%	89.9%	35,779	36,374	72,153
Maryland	12.6%	87.4%	205,158	214,209	419,367
Massachusetts	13.3%	86.7%	300,821	223,620	524,441
Michigan	12.4%	87.6%	343,321	301,119	644,440
Minnesota	11.8%	88.2%	171,790	142,747	314,537
Mississippi	12.8%	87.2%	92,102	62,110	154,212
Missouri	12.0%	88.0%	182,586	159,825	342,411
Montana	10.2%	89.8%	28,497	27,875	56,372
Nebraska	12.4%	87.6%	66,655	50,687	117,342
Nevada	10.9%	89.1%	41,805	68,380	110,185
New Hampshire	11.5%	88.5%	47,255	40,210	87,466
New Jersey	11.9%	88.1%	287,114	248,106	535,219
New Mexico	13.2%	86.8%	64,032	87,287	151,319
New York	13.7%	86.3%	774,517	590,147	1,364,664
North Carolina	12.0%	88.0%	259,327	245,144	504,471
North Dakota	13.1%	86.9%	31,085	17,064	48,149
Ohio	12.2%	87.8%	369,923	306,020	675,943
Oklahoma	12.3%	87.7%	114,039	103,031	217,070
Oregon	10.6%	89.4%	102,620	128,715	231,336
Pennsylvania	11.5%	88.5%	435,939	284,084	720,023
Rhode Island	13.1%	86.9%	51,633	34,061	85,695
South Carolina	12.3%	87.7%	129,311	102,801	232,112
South Dakota	12.0%	88.0%	26,068	18,610	44,677
Tennessee	12.0%	88.0%	179,458	143,337	322,795
Texas	14.9%	85.1%	759,156	670,840	1,429,996
Utah	16.9%	83.1%	115,991	89,996	205,988
Vermont	11.4%	88.6%	25,467	17,744	43,211

	Age Group Proportion		Baseline Enrollment		
	18–24	25+	18–24	25+	18+
Virginia	12.8%	87.2%	269,270	253,314	522,584
Washington	11.7%	88.3%	197,169	231,635	428,804
West Virginia	10.3%	89.7%	50,896	37,602	88,498
Wisconsin	11.7%	88.3%	187,295	153,460	340,755
Wyoming	12.1%	87.9%	18,452	18,434	36,886
United States	13.0%	87.0%	10,365,435	9,226,735	19,592,170

Appendix E

Enrollment Changes: 2000 to 2015

	Numeric		Percentage	
	18–24	25+	18–24	25+
Alabama	12,367	16,274	8.5%	16.9%
Alaska	5,942	4,569	54.4%	21.6%
Arizona	15,508	30,658	10.4%	17.1%
Arkansas	−3,633	9,549	−4.8%	18.2%
California	484,068	226,163	40.8%	16.7%
Colorado	9,956	26,564	7.5%	17.8%
Connecticut	21,856	4,272	21.1%	4.3%
Delaware	2,145	2,332	7.6%	10.1%
Florida	67,932	94,921	16.2%	20.5%
Georgia	28,958	34,125	12.4%	16.9%
Hawaii	13,422	9,741	36.0%	23.2%
Idaho	2,186	12,177	5.1%	35.4%
Illinois	28,398	17,562	6.8%	4.5%
Indiana	88	14,968	0.0%	10.6%
Iowa	−12,296	5,598	−10.3%	8.3%
Kansas	3,195	10,359	3.2%	13.8%
Kentucky	−5,152	9,845	−4.3%	11.3%
Louisiana	8,774	12,565	5.7%	12.2%
Maine	1,451	3,768	4.2%	11.6%
Maryland	42,656	23,932	26.2%	12.6%
Massachusetts	44,831	7,835	17.5%	3.6%
Michigan	2,274	7,959	0.7%	2.7%
Minnesota	2,742	16,390	1.6%	13.0%
Mississippi	−5,802	7,634	−5.9%	14.0%
Missouri	6,977	16,845	4.0%	11.8%
Montana	−410	5,823	−1.4%	26.4%
Nebraska	−508	5,793	−0.8%	12.9%
Nevada	1,980	10,056	5.0%	17.2%
New Hampshire	7,578	5,181	19.1%	14.8%
New Jersey	50,306	16,497	21.2%	7.1%
New Mexico	12,699	19,056	24.7%	27.9%
New York	78,600	−7,749	11.3%	−1.3%
North Carolina	10,518	33,694	4.2%	15.9%
North Dakota	−962	2,145	−3.0%	14.4%
Ohio	9,202	16,181	2.6%	5.6%
Oklahoma	376	14,165	0.3%	15.9%
Oregon	2,301	25,525	2.3%	24.7%
Pennsylvania	8,228	10,823	1.9%	4.0%
Rhode Island	916	943	1.8%	2.8%
South Carolina	3,075	13,205	2.4%	14.7%
South Dakota	−844	2,684	−3.1%	16.9%
Tennessee	15,483	20,755	9.4%	16.9%
Texas	130,253	103,080	20.7%	18.2%
Utah	−514	20,829	−0.4%	30.1%
Vermont	915	2,089	3.7%	13.3%

	Numeric		Percentage	
	18–24	25+	18–24	25+
Virginia	39,596	33,579	17.2%	15.3%
Washington	24,954	47,737	14.5%	26.0%
West Virginia	−6,472	2,820	−11.3%	8.1%
Wisconsin	−2,472	15,470	−1.3%	11.2%
Wyoming	2,644	4,654	16.7%	33.8%
United States	1,196,130	1,046,773	13.0%	12.8%

Appendix F

2015 Comparison Ratios

APPENDIX F: 2015 COMPARISON RATIOS

	Baseline		Baseline Plus		Benchmark	
	18–24	25+	18–24	25+	18–24	25+
Alabama	2.70	0.038	3.24	0.046	3.87	0.073
Alaska	1.20	0.066	1.44	0.080	2.99	0.076
Arizona	2.26	0.063	2.72	0.076	3.70	0.073
Arkansas	2.63	0.034	3.16	0.041	4.39	0.071
California	2.22	0.076	2.66	0.091	2.99	0.076
Colorado	2.52	0.061	3.02	0.073	3.87	0.073
Connecticut	3.18	0.050	3.81	0.059	3.97	0.072
Delaware	3.03	0.051	3.64	0.061	3.83	0.073
Florida	3.06	0.047	3.67	0.056	4.60	0.071
Georgia	2.08	0.045	2.50	0.054	3.56	0.074
Hawaii	2.39	0.061	2.86	0.073	3.50	0.074
Idaho	2.56	0.050	3.07	0.060	3.98	0.072
Illinois	2.60	0.056	3.12	0.067	3.57	0.074
Indiana	2.74	0.041	3.29	0.050	3.82	0.073
Iowa	3.48	0.040	4.17	0.048	4.14	0.072
Kansas	2.85	0.051	3.41	0.061	3.72	0.073
Kentucky	2.56	0.037	3.07	0.045	4.14	0.072
Louisiana	2.33	0.043	2.79	0.052	3.44	0.074
Maine	3.28	0.042	3.94	0.050	4.75	0.071
Maryland	2.89	0.062	3.47	0.075	3.80	0.073
Massachusetts	3.31	0.058	3.97	0.070	3.58	0.074
Michigan	2.95	0.052	3.54	0.063	3.84	0.073
Minnesota	3.07	0.045	3.68	0.054	4.06	0.072
Mississippi	2.45	0.036	2.93	0.043	3.73	0.073
Missouri	2.73	0.045	3.28	0.054	3.97	0.072
Montana	3.30	0.042	3.96	0.050	4.67	0.071
Nebraska	3.12	0.047	3.74	0.057	3.86	0.073
Nevada	2.06	0.050	2.47	0.060	4.39	0.071
New Hampshire	3.36	0.048	4.03	0.058	4.16	0.072
New Jersey	2.95	0.046	3.54	0.056	4.01	0.072
New Mexico	2.20	0.069	2.65	0.083	3.62	0.073
New York	2.90	0.055	3.47	0.066	3.50	0.074
North Carolina	2.57	0.046	3.08	0.055	3.96	0.072
North Dakota	3.36	0.042	4.03	0.050	3.64	0.073
Ohio	2.81	0.045	3.37	0.053	3.93	0.073
Oklahoma	2.59	0.046	3.10	0.055	3.88	0.073
Oregon	2.90	0.051	3.48	0.062	4.50	0.071
Pennsylvania	3.39	0.037	4.07	0.045	4.15	0.072
Rhode Island	3.63	0.055	4.36	0.066	3.63	0.073
South Carolina	2.53	0.039	3.03	0.047	3.89	0.073
South Dakota	2.89	0.038	3.47	0.046	3.99	0.072
Tennessee	2.49	0.037	2.99	0.045	3.97	0.072
Texas	1.93	0.052	2.32	0.063	3.21	0.075
Utah	2.16	0.069	2.60	0.083	2.82	0.077
Vermont	3.77	0.044	4.52	0.052	4.18	0.072

	Baseline		Baseline Plus		Benchmark	
	18–24	25+	18–24	25+	18–24	25+
Virginia	2.65	0.054	3.17	0.065	3.72	0.073
Washington	2.65	0.054	3.18	0.065	4.09	0.072
West Virginia	3.21	0.031	3.86	0.038	4.63	0.071
Wisconsin	3.11	0.045	3.73	0.054	4.07	0.072
Wyoming	2.60	0.050	3.12	0.060	3.93	0.073
United States	2.62	0.052	3.15	0.062	3.69	0.073

Appendix G
2015 Projected Enrollments: 18–24

	Baseline	Baseline Plus	Benchmark	Participation Gap*	Baseline to Baseline Plus
Alabama	157,936	189,523	226,391	68,455	31,587
Alaska	16,863	20,235	41,920	25,057	3,373
Arizona	165,046	198,055	269,641	104,595	33,009
Arkansas	71,381	85,657	119,085	47,703	14,276
California	1,670,784	2,004,941	2,252,489	581,705	334,157
Colorado	142,873	171,448	219,548	76,674	28,575
Connecticut	125,281	150,338	156,352	31,071	25,056
Delaware	30,463	36,556	38,507	8,043	6,093
Florida	487,508	585,010	733,942	246,434	97,502
Georgia	262,039	314,446	447,996	185,957	52,408
Hawaii	50,731	60,878	74,479	23,748	10,146
Idaho	44,643	53,572	69,432	24,789	8,929
Illinois	448,400	538,080	614,866	166,466	89,680
Indiana	210,550	252,660	293,435	82,885	42,110
Iowa	107,117	128,541	127,673	20,555	21,423
Kansas	103,889	124,667	135,937	32,048	20,778
Kentucky	113,324	135,989	183,354	70,029	22,665
Louisiana	162,231	194,678	239,756	77,525	32,446
Maine	35,779	42,935	51,774	15,995	7,156
Maryland	205,158	246,189	269,695	64,537	41,032
Massachusetts	300,821	360,985	325,299	24,478	60,164
Michigan	343,321	411,985	446,893	103,572	68,664
Minnesota	171,790	206,148	227,333	55,543	34,358
Mississippi	92,102	110,522	140,451	48,349	18,420
Missouri	182,586	219,103	265,158	82,572	36,517
Montana	28,497	34,197	40,300	11,803	5,699
Nebraska	66,655	79,986	82,631	15,976	13,331
Nevada	41,805	50,166	89,376	47,571	8,361
New Hampshire	47,255	56,706	58,505	11,250	9,451
New Jersey	287,114	344,536	390,741	103,627	57,423
New Mexico	64,032	76,838	105,210	41,178	12,806
New York	774,517	929,420	934,969	160,452	154,903
North Carolina	259,327	311,193	400,550	141,223	51,865
North Dakota	31,085	37,302	33,672	2,587	6,217
Ohio	369,923	443,908	517,117	147,193	73,985
Oklahoma	114,039	136,847	171,097	57,059	22,808
Oregon	102,620	123,145	159,265	56,645	20,524
Pennsylvania	435,939	523,127	533,184	97,245	87,188
Rhode Island	51,633	61,960	51,633	—	10,327
South Carolina	129,311	155,174	198,989	69,677	25,862
South Dakota	26,068	31,281	35,957	9,890	5,214
Tennessee	179,458	215,350	285,855	106,396	35,892
Texas	759,156	910,988	1,260,299	501,142	151,831
Utah	115,991	139,190	151,354	35,363	23,198
Vermont	25,467	30,561	28,238	2,771	5,093

	Baseline	Baseline Plus	Benchmark	Participation Gap*	Baseline to Baseline Plus
Virginia	269,270	323,124	378,421	109,151	53,854
Washington	197,169	236,603	304,348	107,179	39,434
West Virginia	50,896	61,075	73,267	22,371	10,179
Wisconsin	187,295	224,754	245,205	57,910	37,459
Wyoming	18,452	22,142	27,874	9,422	3,690
United States	10,365,435	12,402,712	14,568,044	4,202,609	2,037,276

*The Participation Gap = Benchmark − Baseline

APPENDIX H

2015 Projected Enrollments: 25+

APPENDIX H: 2015 PROJECTED ENROLLMENTS: 25+

	Baseline	Baseline Plus	Benchmark	Participation Gap*	Baseline to Baseline Plus
Alabama	112,771	135,325	215,011	102,240	22,554
Alaska	25,762	30,914	29,399	3,637	5,152
Arizona	210,395	252,474	242,872	32,477	42,079
Arkansas	62,071	74,486	130,367	68,296	12,414
California	1,583,312	1,899,974	1,583,312	—	316,662
Colorado	175,608	210,729	208,458	32,850	35,122
Connecticut	104,396	125,276	152,517	48,120	20,879
Delaware	25,317	30,381	36,121	10,804	5,063
Florida	557,462	668,955	846,643	289,181	111,492
Georgia	235,930	283,116	386,324	150,394	47,186
Hawaii	51,758	62,109	62,987	11,230	10,352
Idaho	46,604	55,925	67,927	21,324	9,321
Illinois	403,914	484,697	531,172	127,257	80,783
Indiana	156,353	187,623	274,339	117,987	31,271
Iowa	72,944	87,533	130,844	57,900	14,589
Kansas	85,439	102,527	123,356	37,917	17,088
Kentucky	97,130	116,556	187,645	90,516	19,426
Louisiana	115,848	139,018	198,366	82,518	23,170
Maine	36,374	43,649	61,834	25,460	7,275
Maryland	214,209	257,051	250,752	36,542	42,842
Massachusetts	223,620	268,344	282,176	58,556	44,724
Michigan	301,119	361,343	419,918	118,799	60,224
Minnesota	142,747	171,296	227,783	85,036	28,549
Mississippi	62,110	74,532	127,682	65,571	12,422
Missouri	159,825	191,790	258,900	99,075	31,965
Montana	27,875	33,449	47,248	19,374	5,575
Nebraska	50,687	60,825	78,218	27,531	10,137
Nevada	68,380	82,056	97,878	29,497	13,676
New Hampshire	40,210	48,253	60,270	20,060	8,042
New Jersey	248,106	297,727	386,188	138,083	49,621
New Mexico	87,287	104,745	92,504	5,216	17,457
New York	590,147	708,176	788,842	198,695	118,029
North Carolina	245,144	294,173	390,269	145,125	49,029
North Dakota	17,064	20,477	29,778	12,714	3,413
Ohio	306,020	367,224	498,636	192,616	61,204
Oklahoma	103,031	123,637	162,762	59,730	20,606
Oregon	128,715	154,458	178,912	50,196	25,743
Pennsylvania	284,084	340,901	547,583	263,499	56,817
Rhode Island	34,061	40,874	45,518	11,457	6,812
South Carolina	102,801	123,361	189,796	86,994	20,560
South Dakota	18,610	22,331	35,319	16,709	3,722
Tennessee	143,337	172,005	279,027	135,690	28,667
Texas	670,840	805,008	962,998	292,158	134,168
Utah	89,996	107,996	99,315	9,318	17,999
Vermont	17,744	21,292	29,193	11,450	3,549

	Baseline	Baseline Plus	Benchmark	Participation Gap*	Baseline to Baseline Plus
Virginia	253,314	303,977	342,791	89,476	50,663
Washington	231,635	277,962	307,194	75,560	46,327
West Virginia	37,602	45,122	84,976	47,374	7,520
Wisconsin	153,460	184,152	246,311	92,850	30,692
Wyoming	18,434	22,121	26,907	8,473	3,687
United States	9,226,735	11,077,926	13,068,500	3,841,765	1,851,191

*The Participation Gap = Benchmark − Baseline

APPENDIX I

2015 Projected Enrollments: 18+

	Baseline	Baseline Plus	Benchmark	Participation Gap*	Baseline to Baseline Plus
Alabama	270,707	324,848	441,402	170,695	54,141
Alaska	42,624	51,149	71,318	28,694	8,525
Arizona	375,441	450,529	512,513	137,072	75,088
Arkansas	133,453	160,143	249,452	115,999	26,691
California	3,254,096	3,904,915	3,835,801	581,705	650,819
Colorado	318,481	382,177	428,005	109,524	63,696
Connecticut	229,678	275,613	308,869	79,191	45,936
Delaware	55,781	66,937	74,628	18,847	11,156
Florida	1,044,971	1,253,965	1,580,585	535,614	208,994
Georgia	497,969	597,563	834,320	336,351	99,594
Hawaii	102,489	122,987	137,467	34,978	20,498
Idaho	91,247	109,496	137,359	46,112	18,249
Illinois	852,314	1,022,777	1,146,038	293,724	170,463
Indiana	366,903	440,283	567,774	200,871	73,381
Iowa	180,062	216,074	258,517	78,455	36,012
Kansas	189,328	227,194	259,293	69,965	37,866
Kentucky	210,454	252,545	370,999	160,545	42,091
Louisiana	278,080	333,696	438,122	160,043	55,616
Maine	72,153	86,584	113,608	41,455	14,431
Maryland	419,367	503,241	520,447	101,079	83,873
Massachusetts	524,441	629,329	607,475	83,034	104,888
Michigan	644,440	773,328	866,811	222,371	128,888
Minnesota	314,537	377,444	455,116	140,580	62,907
Mississippi	154,212	185,055	268,133	113,920	30,842
Missouri	342,411	410,893	524,058	181,647	68,482
Montana	56,372	67,646	87,548	31,177	11,274
Nebraska	117,342	140,811	160,849	43,507	23,468
Nevada	110,185	132,222	187,254	77,069	22,037
New Hampshire	87,466	104,959	118,775	31,310	17,493
New Jersey	535,219	642,263	776,929	241,710	107,044
New Mexico	151,319	181,583	197,714	46,395	30,264
New York	1,364,664	1,637,596	1,723,811	359,148	272,933
North Carolina	504,471	605,365	790,819	286,348	100,894
North Dakota	48,149	57,779	63,450	15,301	9,630
Ohio	675,943	811,132	1,015,752	339,809	135,189
Oklahoma	217,070	260,484	333,859	116,789	43,414
Oregon	231,336	277,603	338,177	106,841	46,267
Pennsylvania	720,023	864,028	1,080,767	360,744	144,005
Rhode Island	85,695	102,834	97,152	11,457	17,139
South Carolina	232,112	278,535	388,784	156,672	46,422
South Dakota	44,677	53,613	71,276	26,599	8,935
Tennessee	322,795	387,355	564,882	242,086	64,559
Texas	1,429,996	1,715,995	2,223,296	793,300	285,999
Utah	205,988	247,185	250,669	44,681	41,198
Vermont	43,211	51,853	57,432	14,221	8,642

	Baseline	Baseline Plus	Benchmark	Participation Gap*	Baseline to Baseline Plus
Virginia	522,584	627,101	721,212	198,628	104,517
Washington	428,804	514,564	611,543	182,739	85,761
West Virginia	88,498	106,198	158,243	69,745	17,700
Wisconsin	340,755	408,906	491,516	150,761	68,151
Wyoming	36,886	44,263	54,781	17,895	7,377
United States	19,592,170	23,480,638	27,636,544	8,044,374	3,888,467

*The Participation Gap = Benchmark − Baseline

Appendix J

Enrollment Growth Factors

APPENDIX J: ENROLLMENT GROWTH FACTORS 131

	Baseline	Baseline Plus	Benchmark
Alabama	11.8%	34.2%	82.3%
Alaska	32.7%	59.3%	122.1%
Arizona	14.0%	36.8%	55.6%
Arkansas	4.6%	25.6%	95.6%
California	27.9%	53.5%	50.8%
Colorado	13.0%	35.5%	51.8%
Connecticut	12.8%	35.4%	51.7%
Delaware	8.7%	30.5%	45.5%
Florida	18.5%	42.2%	79.2%
Georgia	14.5%	37.4%	91.8%
Hawaii	29.2%	55.0%	73.3%
Idaho	18.7%	42.4%	78.7%
Illinois	5.7%	26.8%	42.1%
Indiana	4.3%	25.1%	61.4%
Iowa	−3.6%	15.7%	38.4%
Kansas	7.7%	29.3%	47.5%
Kentucky	2.3%	22.7%	80.3%
Louisiana	8.3%	30.0%	70.6%
Maine	7.8%	29.4%	69.7%
Maryland	18.9%	42.7%	47.5%
Massachusetts	11.2%	33.4%	28.8%
Michigan	1.6%	21.9%	36.7%
Minnesota	6.5%	27.8%	54.1%
Mississippi	1.2%	21.4%	76.0%
Missouri	7.5%	29.0%	64.5%
Montana	10.6%	32.7%	71.8%
Nebraska	4.7%	25.7%	43.5%
Nevada	12.3%	34.7%	90.8%
New Hampshire	17.1%	40.5%	59.0%
New Jersey	14.3%	37.1%	65.9%
New Mexico	26.6%	51.9%	65.4%
New York	5.5%	26.6%	33.2%
North Carolina	9.6%	31.5%	71.8%
North Dakota	2.5%	23.0%	35.1%
Ohio	3.9%	24.7%	56.1%
Oklahoma	7.2%	28.6%	64.8%
Oregon	13.7%	36.4%	66.2%
Pennsylvania	2.7%	23.3%	54.2%
Rhode Island	2.2%	22.7%	15.9%
South Carolina	7.5%	29.1%	80.1%
South Dakota	4.3%	25.2%	66.4%
Tennessee	12.6%	35.2%	97.1%
Texas	19.5%	43.4%	85.8%
Utah	10.9%	33.1%	35.0%
Vermont	7.5%	29.0%	42.8%
Virginia	16.3%	39.5%	60.5%
Washington	20.4%	44.5%	71.7%
West Virginia	−4.0%	15.2%	71.7%
Wisconsin	4.0%	24.8%	50.0%
Wyoming	24.7%	49.6%	85.1%
United States	10,365,435	12,402,712	4,202,609

APPENDIX K

Funding Scenarios

APPENDIX K: FUNDING SCENARIOS 133

	2000 Actual	2015 Baseline	Baseline Plus	Benchmark
Alabama	$ 1,094,839,000	$ 2,175,814,660	$ 2,610,977,592	$ 3,547,779,236
Alaska	$ 176,494,000	$ 416,291,457	$ 499,549,748	$ 696,532,105
Arizona	$ 865,828,000	$ 1,754,365,879	$ 2,105,239,055	$ 2,394,878,983
Arkansas	$ 605,439,000	$ 1,125,823,477	$ 1,350,988,173	$ 2,104,407,047
California	$ 7,683,934,000	$ 17,467,304,723	$ 20,960,765,667	$ 20,589,773,941
Colorado	$ 719,221,000	$ 1,443,653,648	$ 1,732,384,378	$ 1,940,119,688
Connecticut	$ 699,290,000	$ 1,402,210,797	$ 1,682,652,956	$ 1,885,680,955
Delaware	$ 175,621,000	$ 339,329,867	$ 407,195,840	$ 453,984,197
Florida	$ 2,785,631,000	$ 5,864,181,628	$ 7,037,017,954	$ 8,869,950,401
Georgia	$ 1,560,155,000	$ 3,174,683,710	$ 3,809,620,452	$ 5,319,009,591
Hawaii	$ 342,247,000	$ 785,792,274	$ 942,950,729	$ 1,053,968,972
Idaho	$ 279,290,000	$ 589,038,190	$ 706,845,828	$ 886,713,820
Illinois	$ 2,554,402,000	$ 4,798,099,809	$ 5,757,719,771	$ 6,451,615,765
Indiana	$ 1,226,675,000	$ 2,273,174,027	$ 2,727,808,833	$ 3,517,685,954
Iowa	$ 826,589,000	$ 1,416,234,637	$ 1,699,481,564	$ 2,033,307,168
Kansas	$ 622,198,000	$ 1,190,954,402	$ 1,429,145,282	$ 1,631,064,762
Kentucky	$ 925,506,000	$ 1,682,206,382	$ 2,018,647,659	$ 2,965,478,689
Louisiana	$ 885,055,000	$ 1,703,538,821	$ 2,044,246,586	$ 2,683,972,641
Maine	$ 213,454,000	$ 408,901,850	$ 490,682,220	$ 643,832,616
Maryland	$ 1,042,683,000	$ 2,202,672,985	$ 2,643,207,582	$ 2,733,579,879
Massachusetts	$ 1,046,850,000	$ 2,068,007,601	$ 2,481,609,121	$ 2,395,432,357
Michigan	$ 2,073,579,000	$ 3,744,363,150	$ 4,493,235,780	$ 5,036,396,559
Minnesota	$ 1,280,627,000	$ 2,423,159,374	$ 2,907,791,249	$ 3,506,170,405
Mississippi	$ 917,087,000	$ 1,649,327,953	$ 1,979,193,544	$ 2,867,728,921
Missouri	$ 977,626,000	$ 1,867,218,148	$ 2,240,661,777	$ 2,857,769,501
Montana	$ 138,477,000	$ 272,222,554	$ 326,667,065	$ 422,775,894
Nebraska	$ 473,939,000	$ 881,950,896	$ 1,058,341,076	$ 1,208,951,851
Nevada	$ 305,983,000	$ 610,435,813	$ 732,522,975	$ 1,037,403,293
New Hampshire	$ 96,428,000	$ 200,627,685	$ 240,753,222	$ 272,445,740
New Jersey	$ 1,519,546,000	$ 3,085,452,226	$ 3,702,542,671	$ 4,478,868,645
New Mexico	$ 544,090,000	$ 1,223,687,408	$ 1,468,424,890	$ 1,598,871,779
New York	$ 3,126,582,000	$ 5,860,435,181	$ 7,032,522,217	$ 7,402,764,680
North Carolina	$ 2,293,097,000	$ 4,466,449,328	$ 5,359,739,193	$ 7,001,693,697
North Dakota	$ 187,459,000	$ 341,519,314	$ 409,823,177	$ 450,049,449
Ohio	$ 2,060,555,000	$ 3,804,634,625	$ 4,565,561,550	$ 5,717,294,321
Oklahoma	$ 739,450,000	$ 1,408,404,556	$ 1,690,085,468	$ 2,166,161,172
Oregon	$ 650,142,000	$ 1,313,329,143	$ 1,575,994,971	$ 1,919,880,633
Pennsylvania	$ 1,879,605,000	$ 3,430,981,297	$ 4,117,177,556	$ 5,149,962,301
Rhode Island	$ 150,790,000	$ 273,909,135	$ 328,690,962	$ 310,529,572
South Carolina	$ 812,709,000	$ 1,553,186,689	$ 1,863,824,027	$ 2,601,560,010
South Dakota	$ 130,345,000	$ 241,579,042	$ 289,894,850	$ 385,403,729
Tennessee	$ 984,860,000	$ 1,971,500,203	$ 2,365,800,243	$ 3,450,061,768
Texas	$ 4,093,434,000	$ 8,692,740,325	$ 10,431,288,390	$ 13,515,098,475
Utah	$ 546,774,000	$ 1,077,975,502	$ 1,293,570,603	$ 1,311,801,980
Vermont	$ 63,378,000	$ 121,042,233	$ 145,250,680	$ 160,876,720
Virginia	$ 1,480,258,000	$ 3,058,847,866	$ 3,670,617,439	$ 4,221,478,030
Washington	$ 1,238,035,000	$ 2,649,168,351	$ 3,179,002,022	$ 3,778,137,644
West Virginia	$ 372,505,000	$ 635,737,360	$ 762,884,833	$ 1,136,756,154
Wisconsin	$ 1,075,238,000	$ 1,986,557,439	$ 2,383,868,927	$ 2,865,471,501
Wyoming	$ 139,711,000	$ 309,515,365	$ 371,418,437	$ 459,677,432
United States	$56,683,710,000	$113,438,238,988	$136,125,886,786	$162,090,810,621

Appendix L
Appropriation Increases

APPENDIX L: APPROPRIATION INCREASES

	2000 to 2015 Baseline	Baseline Plus	Benchmark	1985 to 2000 Actual
Alabama	98.7%	138.5%	224.0%	75.0%
Alaska	135.9%	183.0%	294.6%	−25.1%
Arizona	102.6%	143.1%	176.6%	100.3%
Arkansas	86.0%	123.1%	247.6%	102.3%
California	127.3%	172.8%	168.0%	83.3%
Colorado	100.7%	140.9%	169.8%	77.0%
Connecticut	100.5%	140.6%	169.7%	112.0%
Delaware	93.2%	131.9%	158.5%	92.1%
Florida	110.5%	152.6%	218.4%	146.6%
Georgia	103.5%	144.2%	240.9%	134.8%
Hawaii	129.6%	175.5%	208.0%	64.0%
Idaho	110.9%	153.1%	217.5%	129.2%
Illinois	87.8%	125.4%	152.6%	94.3%
Indiana	85.3%	122.4%	186.8%	102.0%
Iowa	71.3%	105.6%	146.0%	114.6%
Kansas	91.4%	129.7%	162.1%	78.0%
Kentucky	81.8%	118.1%	220.4%	113.7%
Louisiana	92.5%	131.0%	203.3%	54.6%
Maine	91.6%	129.9%	201.6%	111.5%
Maryland	111.3%	153.5%	162.2%	95.8%
Massachusetts	97.5%	137.1%	128.8%	47.2%
Michigan	80.6%	116.7%	142.9%	80.9%
Minnesota	89.2%	127.1%	173.8%	77.2%
Mississippi	79.8%	115.8%	212.7%	129.9%
Missouri	91.0%	129.2%	192.3%	115.4%
Montana	96.6%	135.9%	205.3%	28.0%
Nebraska	86.1%	123.3%	155.1%	120.5%
Nevada	99.5%	139.4%	239.0%	224.1%
New Hampshire	108.1%	149.7%	182.5%	91.8%
New Jersey	103.1%	143.7%	194.8%	79.3%
New Mexico	124.9%	169.9%	193.9%	132.4%
New York	87.4%	124.9%	136.8%	22.8%
North Carolina	94.8%	133.7%	205.3%	112.6%
North Dakota	82.2%	118.6%	140.1%	50.7%
Ohio	84.6%	121.6%	177.5%	89.9%
Oklahoma	90.5%	128.6%	192.9%	73.6%
Oregon	102.0%	142.4%	195.3%	108.2%
Pennsylvania	82.5%	119.0%	174.0%	76.7%
Rhode Island	81.6%	118.0%	105.9%	36.6%
South Carolina	91.1%	129.3%	220.1%	60.9%
South Dakota	85.3%	122.4%	195.7%	110.3%
Tennessee	100.2%	140.2%	250.3%	79.8%
Texas	112.4%	154.8%	230.2%	85.7%
Utah	97.2%	136.6%	139.9%	119.2%
Vermont	91.0%	129.2%	153.8%	42.0%

	2000 to 2015 Baseline	Baseline Plus	Benchmark	1985 to 2000 Actual
Virginia	106.6%	148.0%	185.2%	93.0%
Washington	114.0%	156.8%	205.2%	110.2%
West Virginia	70.7%	104.8%	205.2%	59.8%
Wisconsin	84.8%	121.7%	166.5%	64.0%
Wyoming	121.5%	165.8%	229.0%	26.6%
United States	100.1%	140.1%	186.0%	84.5%

Appendix M

2000 Appropriations

State	Expected	Actual	Difference
Alabama	$ 1,383,290,559	$ 1,094,839,000	−26.3%
Alaska	$ 410,844,653	$ 176,494,000	−132.8%
Arizona	$ 1,155,518,185	$ 865,828,000	−33.5%
Arkansas	$ 784,997,548	$ 605,439,000	−29.7%
California	$ 9,106,403,134	$ 7,683,934,000	−18.5%
Colorado	$ 1,171,686,980	$ 719,221,000	−62.9%
Connecticut	$ 577,281,745	$ 699,290,000	17.4%
Delaware	$ 237,483,676	$ 175,621,000	−35.2%
Florida	$ 3,045,478,608	$ 2,785,631,000	−9.3%
Georgia	$ 1,870,924,071	$ 1,560,155,000	−19.9%
Hawaii	$ 464,596,471	$ 342,247,000	−35.7%
Idaho	$ 328,095,010	$ 279,290,000	−17.5%
Illinois	$ 2,523,134,677	$ 2,554,402,000	1.2%
Indiana	$ 1,312,514,894	$ 1,226,675,000	−7.0%
Iowa	$ 836,320,524	$ 826,589,000	−1.2%
Kansas	$ 776,494,927	$ 622,198,000	−24.8%
Kentucky	$ 986,223,009	$ 925,506,000	−6.6%
Louisiana	$ 1,271,313,653	$ 885,055,000	−43.6%
Maine	$ 198,659,381	$ 213,454,000	6.9%
Maryland	$ 1,098,111,254	$ 1,042,683,000	−5.3%
Massachusetts	$ 1,259,187,891	$ 1,046,850,000	−20.3%
Michigan	$ 2,243,936,407	$ 2,073,579,000	−8.2%
Minnesota	$ 1,642,129,841	$ 1,280,627,000	−28.2%
Mississippi	$ 932,965,032	$ 917,087,000	−1.7%
Missouri	$ 1,061,858,620	$ 977,626,000	−8.6%
Montana	$ 230,501,233	$ 138,477,000	−66.5%
Nebraska	$ 432,901,412	$ 473,939,000	8.7%
Nevada	$ 344,752,308	$ 305,983,000	−12.7%
New Hampshire	$ 108,255,235	$ 96,428,000	−12.3%
New Jersey	$ 1,672,700,935	$ 1,519,546,000	−10.1%
New Mexico	$ 681,561,764	$ 544,090,000	−25.3%
New York	$ 4,617,934,114	$ 3,126,582,000	−47.7%
North Carolina	$ 2,318,997,713	$ 2,293,097,000	−1.1%
North Dakota	$ 235,151,992	$ 187,459,000	−25.4%
Ohio	$ 2,055,130,228	$ 2,060,555,000	0.3%
Oklahoma	$ 800,989,856	$ 739,450,000	−8.3%
Oregon	$ 706,232,703	$ 650,142,000	−8.6%
Pennsylvania	$ 2,145,612,236	$ 1,879,605,000	−14.2%
Rhode Island	$ 209,941,381	$ 150,790,000	−39.2%
South Carolina	$ 1,249,653,813	$ 812,709,000	−53.8%
South Dakota	$ 141,624,912	$ 130,345,000	−8.7%
Tennessee	$ 1,263,529,145	$ 984,860,000	−28.3%
Texas	$ 5,041,321,784	$ 4,093,434,000	−23.2%
Utah	$ 688,638,059	$ 546,774,000	−25.9%
Vermont	$ 92,692,355	$ 63,378,000	−46.3%
Virginia	$ 1,762,066,187	$ 1,480,258,000	−19.0%
Washington	$ 1,386,274,546	$ 1,238,035,000	−12.0%
West Virginia	$ 478,960,238	$ 372,505,000	−28.6%
Wisconsin	$ 1,290,496,513	$ 1,075,238,000	−20.0%
Wyoming	$ 235,021,080	$ 139,711,000	−68.2%
United States	$66,870,392,495	$56,683,710,000	−18.0%

References

Albright, B. N. (1998). *The transition from business as usual to funding for results: State efforts to integrate performance measures in the higher education budgetary process.* Denver, CO: State Higher Education Executive Officers Association [commissioned paper].

Astin, A. (1998). The changing American college student: Thirty-year trends (1966–1996). *Review of Higher Education,* 21(2), pp. 115–135.

Bailey, A. A., and Mingle, J. R. (2003). *The adult learning gap: Why states need to change their policies toward adult learners.* Denver, CO: Education Commission of the States.

Bloom, A. (1987). *The closing of the American mind.* New York, NY: Simon and Schuster.

Bloom, D., Canning, D., and Sevilla, J. (2002). *The demographic dividend: A new perspective on the economic consequences of population change* (p. 3). Santa Monica, CA: RAND,Corp. RB 5065.

Bowen, H. (1977). Goals: The intended outcomes of higher education. In Bess, J. L., & Webster, D. S. (Eds.), *ASHE reader on foundations of American higher education* (2nd ed., pp. 23–37). Boston, MA: Pearson Custom Publishing.

Bowen, H. (1980). *The costs of higher education: How much do colleges and universities spend per student and how much should they spend?* (pp. 19–20). San Francisco, CA: Jossey-Bass.

Burke, J. C., and Serban, A. M. (1997). *Performance funding and budgeting for public higher education: Current status and future prospects.* Albany, NY: Rockefeller Institute of Government.

Callan, P. M., and Finney, J. E. (Eds.). (1997). *Public and private financing of higher education: Shaping public policy for the future* (p. xi). Phoenix, AZ: American Council on Education and Oryx Press.

Carnegie Commission on Higher Education. (1973). *Higher education: Who pays? Who benefits? Who should pay?* (p. 3). New York, NY: McGraw-Hill.

Cauchon, D. (2003, June 23). Bad moves, not economy, behind busted state budgets. *USA Today,* pp. 1A–2A.

Clark, R. B. (1983). *The higher education system: Academic organization in cross-national perspective.* Berkeley, CA: University of California Press.

Cunningham, A. F., and Wellman, J. A. (2001). *Beneath the surface: A statistical analysis of the major variables associated with state grades in Measuring Up 2000.* San Jose, CA: National Center for Public Policy and Higher Education, Report No. 01–04.

DeVol, R. C. (1999). *America's high-tech economy.* Santa Monica, CA: The Milken Institute.

Ewell, P. T., and Jones, D. (1994). *Pointing the way: Indicators as policy tools in education.* Denver, CO: Education Commission of the States [commissioned paper].

Foster, G. (1986). *Financial statement analysis* (2nd ed., p. 71). Englewood Cliffs, NJ: Prentice Hall.

Gladieux, L. (2002). Federal student aid in historical perspective. In Heller, D. (Ed.), *Condition of access: Higher education for lower income students* (p. 47). Westport, CT: Praeger.

Gold, S. D. (1995). State fiscal problems and policies. In Gold, S. D. (Ed.), *The fiscal crisis of the states: Lessons for the future* (pp. 6–36). Washington, DC: Georgetown University Press.

Goodstein, L. D., and Burke, W. W. (1995). Creating successful organizational change. In Burke, W. W. (Ed.), *Managing organizational change* (p. 10). New York, NY: The American Management Association.

The Grapevine. (2003). Online publication (http://www.coe.ilstu.edu/grapevine/Historicaldata.htm), Illinois State University.

Gratz v. Bollinger (000 U.S. Supreme Court 02-516 (2003)).

Hauptman, A. M. (1997). Financing American higher education in the 1990s. In Yeager, J. L., Nelson, G. M., Potter, E. A., Weidman, J. C., and Zullo, T. G. (Eds.), *ASHE reader on finance in higher education* (2nd ed., pp. 118–119). Boston, MA: Pearson Custom Publishing.

Heller, D. (2001a). Technology and the future of higher education policy. In Heller, D. (Ed.), *The states and public higher education policy: Affordability, access and accountability* (pp. 243–258). Baltimore, MD: The Johns Hopkins University Press.

Heller, D. (2001b). Trends in the affordability of public colleges and universities: The contradiction of increasing prices and increasing enrollment. In Heller, D. (Ed.), *The states and public higher education policy: Affordability, access and accountability* (pp. 11–38). Baltimore, MD: The Johns Hopkins University Press.

Hossler, D., Lund, J. P., Ramin, J., Westfall, S., and Irish, S. (1997). State funding for higher education. *Journal of Higher Education,* 69(2), p. 173.

Hovey, H. (1999, July). *State spending for higher education in the next decade: The battle to sustain current support.* San Jose, CA: The National Center for Public Policy and Higher Education, Report No. 99-3.

Immerwahr, J., and Foleno, T. (2000). *Great expectations: How the public and parents—White, African American and Hispanic—view higher education.* San Jose, CA: The National Center for Public Policy and Higher Education, Report No. 00-2.

Institute for Higher Education Policy. (1999). *The tuition puzzle: Putting the pieces together.* Washington, DC: The Institute for Higher Education Policy.

Jones, D., Ewell, P., and McGuinness, A. C. (1998, December). *The challenges and opportunities facing higher education: An agenda for policy research.* San Jose, CA: The National Center for Public Policy and Higher Education [commissioned paper].

Kane, T. J., and Rouse, C. E. (1999). The community college: Educating students at the margin between college and work. In Yeager, J. L., Nelson, G. M., Potter, E. A., Weidman, J. C., and Zullo, T. G. (Eds.), *ASHE reader on finance in higher education* (2nd ed., pp. 86–89). Boston, MA: Pearson Custom Publishing.

Layzell, D. T. (1998, March). Linking performance to funding outcomes for public institutions of higher education: The U.S. experience. *European Journal of Education*, 33(1), pp. 103–111.

Martinez, M. C., Farias, J., and Arellano, E. (2002). State higher education report cards: What's in a grade? *Review of Higher Education*, 26(1), pp. 1–18.

Martinez, M. C., (2002). New Mexico Case Report: The state role in a climate of autonomy. New York: New York University: The Alliance for International Higher Education Policy Studies http://www.nyu.edu/iesp/aiheps/research.html

McGuinness, A., and Jones, D. (2003). *Narrowing the gap in educational attainment to improve state performance.* Denver, CO: Education Commission of the States.

Mingle, J. R. (1988). Effective coordination of higher education: What is it? Why is it so difficult to achieve? *Issues in Higher Education*, 23.

Mingle, J. R. (2000, September). *Higher education's future in the "corporatized" economy* [commissioned paper]. Washington, DC: Association of Governing Boards of Universities and Colleges.

Mingle, J. R. and Epper, R. M. (1996). *Planning and management for a changing environment.* Jossey Bass, Inc.

Mintzberg, H. (1994). *The rise and fall of strategic planning* (pp. 1–29). New York: The Free Press.

Morrison, J. L., and Wilson, I. (1997). Analyzing environments and developing scenarios for uncertain times. In Peterson, M. W., Dill, D. D., and Mets, L. A. (Eds.), *Planning and management for a changing environment* (pp. 204–229). San Francisco, CA: Jossey Bass Publishers.

Mortenson, T. (2002). *Chance for college by age 19.* Unpublished spreadsheet report from Postsecondary Education Opportunity. Oskaloosa, IA: Postsecondary Education Opportunity.

National Center for Educational Statistics. (2001a). *Residence and migration of all freshmen students in degree granting institutions by state, 1998.* Integrated Postsecondary Data System, Table 204.

National Center for Educational Statistics. (2001b). *Fall enrollments in colleges and universities.* Higher Education General Information Survey. Integrated Postsecondary Education Data System, Table 191.

National Center for Educational Statistics. (December 2003). *Participation in technology-based postcompulsory education.* Issue Brief 2004-020. Washington, DC: The United States Department of Education, Institute of Education Sciences.

The National Center for Public Policy and Higher Education. (2000). *Measuring Up 2000: The state-by-state report card for higher education.* San Jose, CA: The National Center for Public Policy and Higher Education.

Newman, F. (1987). *Choosing quality* [commissioned paper]. Denver, CO: Education Commission of the States.

Oberlin, J. L. (1996, Summer). The financial mythology of information technology: Developing a new financial game plan. *Cause/EFFECT*, pp. 362–370.

Perlmann, J. and Waters, M. C. (Eds.). (2002). *The new race question: How the census counts multiracial individuals* (pp. 1–27). New York, NY: Russell Sage Foundation.

Perna, L. W. (2003). The private benefits of higher education: An examination of the earnings premium. *Research in Higher Education*, 44(4), p. 454.

Privateer, P. M. (1999, Jan/Feb). Academic technology and the future of higher education: Strategic paths taken and not taken. *Journal of Higher Education*, 70(1), pp. 60–79.

Research Associates of Washington. (2003). *College and university higher education price index: 2003*. Arlington, VA, www.rschassoc.com/ inflation.html

Richardson, R. C. (2002, January). *New Jersey case report.* New York University, Alliance for International Higher Education Policy Studies (AIHEPS), http://www.nyu.edu/iesp/aiheps/research.html

Ruppert, S. S. (1996). The politics of remedy: State legislative views on higher education. Washington, DC: National Education Association.

Ruppert, S. S. (2001). *Where we go from here: State legislative views on higher education in the new millennium.* Washington, DC: National Education Association.

Selingo, J. (2003, February 28). The disappearing state in public higher education. *Chronicle of Higher Education* [Online]. Available: www.chronicle.com/free/v49/i25/25a02201.htm

Senge, P. (1990). *The fifth discipline.* New York: Doubleday Books, pp. 141–142.

Taylor, T. (Speaker). (1996). *A history of the U.S. economy in the 20th century* (cassette recording: course no. 529, lectures 2 and 3). Chantilly, VA: The Teaching Company.

The Texas Higher Education Coordinating Board. (2002). *Closing the gap: The Texas Higher Education Plan.* Austin, TX. Au.

Thurow, L. C. (200). Building wealth: The new rules for individuals, companies, and nations in a knowledge-based economy. New York: Harper Business, pp. 160–165.

Trombley, W. (1999). Performance based budgeting: South Carolina's new plan mired in detail and confusion. *CrossTalk.* San Jose, CA: The National Center for Public Policy and Higher Education, 6(1).

United Health Foundation. (2002). *State health rankings, 2002,* www.unitedhealthfoundation.org

United States Department of Education. (2003). Information on No Child Left Behind retrieved from www.ed.gov/nclb/overview/ intro/html on 11/25/03.

Vernez, G., Krop, R. A., and Rydell, C. P. (1999). *Closing the education gap: Benefits and costs.* Santa Monica, CA: RAND, MR-1036-EDU.

Weick, K. (1984). Small wins: Redefining the scale of social problems. *American Psychologist*, 39(1), pp. 40–43.

Notes

a. Throughout the book, the terms "higher education," "postsecondary education," and "college" are used interchangeably to mean education and training beyond high school, including two- and four-year, public and private.
1. The National Center for Educational Statistics provides information on college enrollment by age. NCES Table 176, total fall enrollment in degree-granting institutions, 1999, has numerical figures for enrollment by age. The author's calculation for those under 18 attending postsecondary education, in Fall 2000, was 2.6 percent.
2. A Pearson correlation was run between participation rates and the following measures: associate, bachelor, and graduate attainment in the 25 and older population; family income; poverty; degree completion; and voting percentages. The level of significance was set at .05. All measures were from U.S. Census 2000 (www.census.gov) except degree completion and voting percentages. These two measures were taken from Measuring Up 2002, the National Center for Public Policy and Higher Education's national report card (www.highereducation.org).
3. In the 1950 and subsequent censuses, college students were enumerated where they lived while attending college; whereas in earlier censuses, they generally were enumerated at their parental homes. Instructions mailed with the census questionnaire specified that enrollment in a trade or business school, company training, or tutoring were not to be included as enrollment unless the course would be accepted for credit at a regular college. The full definition of participation for Census 2000 can be obtained from www.census.gov, Summary File 3, Table PCT24.
4. Appendix A displays postsecondary participation for 18- to 24-year-olds and those 25 and older. The percentage of each age group represented in postsecondary education, by state, can be calculated by dividing each age group's absolute participation by total participation. States such as Maryland and Nevada show a majority of students belong to the 25 and older age group.

5. State-by-state information on median family income from www.census.gov/qfd, State and County QuickFacts.
6. State-by-state information on racial and ethnic composition of the population from www.census.gov/qfd, State and County QuickFacts.
7. State-by-state information from 2000 decennial census, Summary File 3, Table P37: Sex by educational attainment for the population 25 years and over, 2000.
8. See the reference for McGuinness and Jones (2003) in the reference section of this book for source. McGuinness and Jones provide the highlights for 2000 enacted Senate Bill 653, which called for a Compact for the Future of West Virginia linking higher education to the future of the state and enacting specific provisions to ensure sufficient capacity at community colleges.
9. Since enrollment projections for 2015 were contrasted with 2000 participation data, the funding analysis also uses 2000 funding as the point of comparison for 15 years past and 15 years in the future.
10. See the reference for the Grapevine in the reference section of this book for website information. The Grapevine, at Illinois State University, tracks yearly state appropriations. These appropriations include student aid and operating costs. Enrollment projections in the previous chapter were constructed relative to 2000 enrollments, and funding projections also are constructed relative to actual appropriations for 2000.
11. A compounded annual inflation rate is distinct from an average annual growth rate. A compounded annual inflation calculation specifies the average inflation rate over a given period, whereas an annual growth rate is a simple linear calculation of growth. The concept of compounding and the effect of inflation can be captured by calculating future value. The future value is calculated by the formula:

$$\text{Future Value} = PV * (1 + r)^n$$

PV = current dollar value;
r = the interest or inflation rate; and
n = the number of years into the future.

Any variable can be determined if the other three variables in the equation are known.

12. See the reference for the Grapevine for website information. The Grapevine provides 1985 appropriation data and 2000 appropriation data for higher education, by state. These data sets

were compared and a historical 15-year change calculated for purposes of Table 5.2.
13. The calculation for comparing 2015 baseline projections with 2000 enrollments for the 18–24 age group was obtained by subtracting the total in Appendix G from the total in Appendix A, for this age group.
14. The calculation for comparing 2015 baseline projections with 2000 enrollments for the 25+ age group was obtained by subtracting the total in Appendix H from the total in Appendix A, for this age group.
15. NCES (2001). Table 173. The table provides enrollments for 1979 and 1999. Author's calculations show the 1999 share of enrollment by sector as follows: private four-year, 21.5 percent; public four-year, 40.5 percent; private two-year, 1.7 percent; and public two-year, 36.5 percent.
16. The Chronicle of Higher Education (August 30, 2002). Almanac, 2002–3. Washington, DC: The Chronicle of Higher Education, XLIX (1). The 2002–2003 Almanac provides 1999 state enrollment by sector and level. Percentage attendance by sector and level are taken from the numerical information in the Almanac and are the author's calculations. Author's calculations for Fall 1999 enrollment by sector for the nation are as follows: public two-year, 36.3 percent; public four-year, 40.5 percent; private two-year, 1.7 percent; and private four-year, 21.5 percent.
17. NCES (2001). Table 173. See note 15.
18. NCES (2001). Table 176. Author's calculations show that 79.1 percent of those 25 and older enrolled in a community college are part-time status, compared with 44.6 percent for students who fall between the ages of 18–24.
19. Graduate and professional students as a percentage of total enrollment calculated from the *Chronicle of Higher Education Almanac, 2002–2003*. The national percentage is 14.1 percent. Graduate and professional student enrollment as a percentage of the total enrollment population for the sample case study states include the following: Massachusetts, 23.1 percent; Georgia, 16.2 percent; Colorado, 16 percent; Virginia, 15.6 percent; Washington, 8.7 percent; and North Dakota, 7.7 percent.
20. NCES (2001). Fall Enrollment Survey, 1998. Integrated Postsecondary Data System, Table 205. According to NCES, Table 205, North Dakota's net migration into the state's higher education institutions was 1,414 in 1998.
21. See note 16.

Index

Access
  and technology, 32
  Who has it?, 80
Accountability
  and efficiency, 86
Act 86, 359
Affirmative Action, 78
Affordability, 78, 93
  policies, 101
Age group proportions, 18, 35
Age structure, 18
  and participation, 17
Alaska, 21–28, 35, 36, 51, 52, 56
  18–24 enrollment, 2015, 56
  25+ participation gap, 2015, 51
Albright, 86
Arizona, 29
  25+ enrollment, 2015, 57
  25+ participation gap, 2015, 52
Arkansas, 3, 37, 38, 40–45, 52, 53, 57, 58, 65, 69–73
  18–24 enrollment, 2015, 56
  18+ enrollment, 2015, 58
  18+ participation gap, 2015, 53
  25+ enrollment, 2015, 57
  25+ participation gap, 2015, 52
  funding projections, 72
Assessment. *See also* Accountability
Astin, 92

Bailey and Mingle, 88, 101
Baseline
  purpose of, 43
Baseline Comparison Ratios
  formula, 42
Baseline Plus, 55
  definition, 48
  formula, 55
Baseline Scenario
  definition, 33
  equation, 39
  future enrollment, 39
Benchmark, 49–54
  purpose of, 49
Benchmark Enrollment
  formula, 49
Bloom, 8, 9
Bloom, Canning, and Sevilla, 9, 18, 38
Bowen, 9, 11, 74
Burke and Serban, 86
Business. *See* Higher education or Workforce preparation

California, 3, 21–25, 28–30, 35–45, 47, 48, 49, 52–54, 57–59, 64, 65, 70, 72, 73, 81, 84, 86
  18+ enrollment, 2015, 58
  18+ participation gap, 2015, 53
  funding projections, 93
  Master Plan, 81
  25+ enrollment, 2015, 57
  25+ participation gap, 2015, 52
California Community College, 29, 81
California State University system, 81
Callan and Finney, 1, 2
Capacity-building
  and demographics, 82
Carnegie Commission on Higher Education, 8
Caseload growth. *See* Enrollment
Cauchon, 5
Census, 2, 3, 17
Chance for college, 100
Child well-being, 13
  and attainment, 13
Civic participation
  and attainment, 13
Closing the Gap, 8
Collaboration
  with K-12, 93
Colorado, 95, 99–101
  case study, 95
  Demographics, 95
Communication
  between institutions, 93
Community College, 82
Comparison ratio, 20–30
  current, national, 21
  equation, 21
Completion. *See* Educational attainment
Connecticut, 21–23, 26–28, 30
Consumer Price Index (CPI), 62, 66–68
Cost efficient, 85
Costs of Higher Education, The, 74
Crime
  and education, 13
Cunningham and Wellman, 4, 25

Decennial census, 33, *See* Census
Degree
  associate, 12, 13
  bachelor, 12, 13
  doctoral, 12, 13
  professional, 12, 13
Demographics
  and capacity building, 82

147

148 INDEX

Colorado, 95
Georgia, 95
Massachusetts, 95
North Dakota, 95
U.S., 95
Virginia, 95
Washington, 95
DeVol, 10

Economic development state, 10, 17, 32
Economic engine
 and higher education, 92
Economies of scale
 and efficiency, 85
Educational attainment
 lifetime earnings, 13
 and participation, 13
 policy perspective, 13
Efficiency, 93
 and tuition, 85
18+ participation gap, 2015
 Arkansas, 53
 California, 53
 Kentucky, 53
 Maryland, 53
 Massachusetts, 53
 Mississippi, 53
 Rhode Island, 53
 Tennessee, 53
 Utah, 53
 West Virginia, 53
18-to-24 participation, 17
Elementary and Secondary Education
 Act, 47
Enrollment
 growth factor, 63
 and population, 23
Enrollment 18-24, 2015
 Alaska, 56
 Arkansas, 56
 Georgia, 56
 Iowa, 56
 Massachusetts, 56
 Nevada, 56
 North Dakota, 56
 Rhode Island, 56
 Texas, 56
 Vermont, 56
Enrollment, 18+, 2015
 Arkansas, 53
 California, 53
 Kentucky, 53
 Maryland, 53
 Massachusetts, 53
 Mississippi, 53
 Rhode Island, 53
 Tennessee, 53
 Utah, 53
 West Virginia, 53
Enrollment, 25+, 2015
 Alaska, 57
 Arizona, 57
 Arkansas, 57
 California, 57

Kentucky, 57
Mississippi, 57
New Mexico, 57
Tennessee, 57
Utah, 57
West Virginia, 57
Enrollment demand
 future factors, 31
Enrollment patterns, 41, 83
Enrollment projections, 31
 process of, 33
Enrollment supply, 77–89
Expected participation rate, 24

Financial aid
 and demand, 78
Financial ratio analysis
 definition, 20
 and higher education, 20
Florida
 Profile, 19
Foster, 20
Funding
 base level, 63
 future of, 68–74
 projection formulas, 69
Funding projections
 Arkansas, 70
 California, 70
 Idaho, 70
 Michigan, 70
 New York, 70

Geographical location
 and participation rate, 25
Georgia, 56, 95, 99–101
 18–24 enrollment, 2015, 56
 case study, 96
 demographics, 95
GI Bill, 8
Gladieux, 14
Goals
 state improvement, 55
Gold, 61, 63, 68
Goodstein and Burke, 15
Governance
 and accountability, 86
 institutional, 81
Grapevine, The, 61, 63, 71
Gratz v. Bollinger, 78

Halstead, 66
Hauptman, 62
Hawaii, 35, 36
Health
 and attainment, 13
Heller, 32, 77
Higher education, 8
 access, 8
 American Colonial times, 8
 and income, 12
 outcomes, 11
 public and private benefits, 8–14
 and workforce training, 14

INDEX   149

Higher Education Price Index (HEPI), 62
   definition, 69
HOPE scholarship, 96
Hossler, Lund, Ramin, Westfall, and Irish, 63
Hovey, 32, 61, 62, 68, 75

Idaho, 3, 37, 38, 40–45, 64, 65, 70, 71, 72, 73
   funding projections, 72
Illinois
   Profile, 19
Immerwahr and Foleno, 1
Improvement goals, 54
Industry. *See* Higher education and Workforce preparation
Inflation, 5, 66–75, 77
Institutional appropriations, 88
Interactive Television, 87
Internet, 87
Iowa
   18–24 enrollment, 2015, 56

Jefferson, Thomas, 8

Kane and Rouse, 81, 82
Kentucky
   18+ enrollment, 2015, 58
   18+ participation gap, 2015, 53
   25+ enrollment, 2015, 57
   25+ participation gap, 2015, 52
Key Issues in Higher Education Series, 2
Knowledge-Based Economy, 92

Lifetime earnings
   and educational attainment, 12, 77
   gap, 12, 77
Lottery
   scholarship program, 83

Martinez, M. C., 83, 84
Martinez, Farias, and Arellano, 4, 25
Maryland, 18, 53
   18+ enrollment, 2015, 58
   18+ participation gap, 2015, 53
Massachusetts, 53, 95, 97, 100–101
   Case study, 97
   Demographics, 95
   18–24 enrollment, 2015, 56
   18+ enrollment, 2015, 58
   18+ participation gap, 2015, 53
Maximum future enrollment. *See* Benchmark
McGuinness and Jones, 13, 88
Measuring Up 2000, 26
Median family income, 26, 29
   and participation, 26, 29
Michigan, 35–38, 40, 42, 43, 45, 65, 70–73
   funding projections, 72
Midwestern states
   and population, 36
Milken Institute, 10
Mill, John Stuart, 8

Minimum future enrollment. *See* Baseline
Minorities
   and enrollment, 78
Mintzberg, 15
Mississippi, 52, 53, 57, 58
   18+ enrollment, 2015, 58
   18+ participation gap, 2015, 53
   25+ enrollment, 2015, 57
   25+ participation gap, 2015, 52
Morrison and Wilson, 48
Mortenson, 100

National Center for Educational Statistics, 27, 87
National Center for Public Policy and Higher Education (NCPPHE), 4, 25, 26
Nevada, 18, 51, 56, 84
   18–24 enrollment, 2015, 56
New Hampshire, 81
New Jersey, 3, 37, 63, 81, 97
New Mexico, 29, 35, 37, 38, 40–43, 45, 57, 83, 84, 96
   25+ enrollment, 2015, 57
   25+ participation gap, 2015, 52
New Mexico Commission on Higher Education, 83
New York, 3, 36–38, 40–45, 65, 70, 72, 73, 81, 84
   funding projections, 72
North Carolina, 87
North Dakota, 98–102
   case study, 98
   demographics, 95
   18–24 enrollment, 2015, 56
Northeastern states
   and population, 36
Numerical Changes in Enrollment
   formula, 41

Oberlin, 87
Open University
   England, 87

Participation
   and completion, 16
   median family income. *See* Higher education benefits
Participation Gap
   definition, 66
   formula, 66
Participation rate
   current, national, 17
   definition, 16
   expected, formula, 24
   expected, state, 24
   formula, 17
   state factors, 25
Pell Grant, 8
Pennsylvania, 36, 37, 40, 41, 42, 43, 45, 81
Percentage Changes in Enrollment
   formula, 41
Perlmann and Waters, 2
Planning, 18, 53

Policy
    questions, 19
    tools, 32
Postsecondary participation definition, 17
Poverty. *See* Health
President's Commission on Higher
    Education, 8
Preventable diseases. *See* Health
Price and quantity
    supply and demand, 78
Privateer, 32
Private institutions, 78
Public consumption, 14
Public investment, 14

RAND, 14
Recruitment, 32
Regional outcomes, 53
Religious culture
    and post secondary participation, 27
Research Associates of Washington, 66
Return on assets
    definition, 20
Rhode Island, 22, 23, 26, 27, 28, 35, 36, 51,
        53, 56, 58
    18–24 enrollment, 2015, 36
    18+ enrollment, 2015, 36
    18+ participation gap, 2015, 51
Richardson, 81
Ruppert, 10, 12, 25, 32, 78, 87, 91, 92, 101

Selingo, 88
Senge, 15
Singapore, 14
Smoking. *See* Health
South Carolina, 86
    and performance based funding, 86
South Dakota, 63
Southern states
    and participation gap, 53
    and population, 34
State context
    and performance, 25
Student
    adult student population, 4
    traditional student population, 4
Supply
    and state policy, 78
Supreme Court, 78

Taylor, 32
Technology
    and access, 32
    and accountability, 86
    and higher education efficiency, 32
    and supply, 87
Tennessee
    18+ enrollment, 2015, 36
    18+ participation gap, 2015, 51
    25+ enrollment, 2015, 57
    25+ participation gap, 2015, 52
Texas
    18–24 enrollment, 2015, 56

Texas Higher Education Coordinating
    Board, 8
Thurow, Lester, 14
Trombley, 86
20% improvement. *See also* Baseline Plus
25+ participation, 27
25+ participation gap, 2015
    Alaska, 52
    Arizona, 52
    Arkansas, 52
    California, 52
    Kentucky, 52
    Mississippi, 52
    New Mexico, 52
    Tennessee, 52
    Utah, 52
    West Virginia, 52
Two-year sector, 29. *See also* Community
    College

United Health Foundation, 13
United States
    enrollment by sector and level, 83
United States Department of Labor
    Bureau of Labor Statistics, 66
University of California, 81
University of Texas at Brownsville, 67
U.S. Bureau of the Census, 15
U.S. Department of Education, 72
USA Today, 5
Utah, 22, 23, 24, 25, 26, 27, 28, 29, 35, 52,
        53, 57, 58
    18+ enrollment, 2015, 58
    18+ participation gap, 2015, 53
    25+ enrollment, 2015, 57
    25+ participation gap, 2015, 52

Vermont
    18–24 enrollment, 2015, 51
Vernez, Krop and Rydell, 13, 14
Violent crimes. *See* Health
Virginia, 95, 98, 99, 100, 101
    case study, 98
    demographics, 95
Voting
    and attainment, 13

Washington, 29, 82, 99–101
    case study, 99
    demographics, 95
Weick, 54
West Virginia, 21, 22, 23, 27, 28, 29, 30–33,
        35, 52, 53
    18+ enrollment, 2015, 58
    18+ participation gap, 2015, 53
    Legislature, 29
    25+ enrollment, 2015, 57
    25+ participation gap, 2015, 52
Western states, 39
    and participation gap, 52
    and population, 36
Workforce preparation
    and educational attainment, 13, 102